IRRATIONAL THINGS

Mu Tao was born in Langfang, Hebei Province in 1963 and raised mostly in nearby Xuanhua. He currently lives in Xi'an (formerly the ancient capital city, Chang'an). Mr Mu studied at the prestigious Writing School at Northwest University and serves as editor of the *Meiwen* ("Elegant Prose") literary journal. His essay collections include a study of the novelist Tie Ning and *Social Customs of Bygone Days*, which was awarded the Lu Xun Prize. Elected Vice President of the China Prose Association in April 2021, he is a noted gourmet and antiquary as well.

This book is part of Shaanxi Stories, a series of translated works by acclaimed authors from the Shaanxi province of China, produced by Valley Press in collaboration with Northwest University, Xi'an. The series editors are Hu Zongfeng and Robin Gilbank. Other books in the series:

MOUNTAIN STORIES, Ye Guangqin
HOW OLD DAN BECAME A TREE, Yang Zhengguang
THE EARTHEN GATE, Jia Pingwa
THE BLOOD RED SUN, Wu Keijing
THE HOWL OF THE WOLF, Hong Ke
THE WILD LAND, Jia Pingwa
SUN PALACE, Ye Guangqin
THE HOUR OF THE LOCUST, Yang Zhengguang

Irrational Things

Mu Tao

*translated by Hu Zongfeng
and Robin Gilbank*

Valley Press

First published in 2022 by Valley Press
Woodend, The Crescent, Scarborough, YO11 2PW
www.valleypressuk.com

ISBN 978-1-912436-65-1
Cat. no. VP0186

Copyright © Mu Tao 2022

The right of Mu Tao to be identified as the
author of this work has been asserted in accordance with
the Copyright, Designs and Patents Act 1988.

All rights reserved. No part of this publication may be
reproduced, stored in or introduced into a retrieval system,
or transmitted in any form, by any means (electronic,
mechanical, photocopying, recording or otherwise) without
prior written permission from the rights holders.

A CIP record for this book is available from the British Library.

Cover and text design by Peter Barnfather.
Cover art: rubbing from a Han dynasty tile (Shaanxi).
Series edited by Hu Zongfeng and Robin Gilbank.

Printed and bound in Great Britain
by Clays Ltd, Elcograf S.p.A.

Contents

Mu Tao and His Stories
- I. 9
- II. 10

Taking a Stroll in Chang'an City
- I. AT THE FOOT OF THE CITY WALL 13
- II. THE ZHONGNAN MOUNTAINS 16
- III. THE FISH IN THE LAKE 18
- IV. CULTURE 23
- V. GUESTS 25
- VI. RECORDS OF GREAT EVENTS 26
- VII. TWO MEN 27
- VIII. IRRATIONAL THINGS 28

Men's Mistakes 31

Splendid Folk Customs 35

Fine Pink Hands 40

Bunny Love 45

An Era without Nursery Rhymes 50

Knocking a Wooden Fish 53

Culture has Blood and Flesh 56

Civilised People 59

The Servers within the Organs of the Human Body 61

Turning to Look Back 64

Eradicating Desire 67
Thieves in the Heart 72
Knowing How to Talk 76
Price and Cost 79
Crying Uncle 83
Two Reflections on the Great Helmsman
    I. THE REVELATION OF THE LEADER'S BUST 86
    II. THE FAITH OF CAB DRIVERS 88
To Write Prose is to Speak Human Words 91
In What Kind of House Did the Jade Emperor Live? 96
A Lost Quarter Hour of My Life 102
Tie Ning in Close-up 108
A Pair of Straw Sandals 111
Space 112
My Two Legs Can Surely Outpace the Chinese 115
Lonesome to the Limit: A Cautionary Tale from the 1990s 118
The Country Bumpkin: Early Reflections on Jia Pingwa 121
A Response from Mu Tao 127
Positions and Ideas 136

Mu Tao and His Stories

by Jia Pingwa

I.

I am the Editor-in-Chief of the prose magazine *Meiwen*, and Mu Tao, who is my deputy, transferred to Xi'an from Hebei Province. He is a man of wisdom and jocularity. One day, we visited a county outside Xi'an. While passing the northern slopes of the Qinling Mountains, he sighed with emotion: "You Shaanxi people really are modest. You use the suffix *ling* – 'ridge' – to describe such a great mountain range." I knew he was about to malign my homeland again, so I interjected: "Not as much as you Hebei folk. The capital of your province, Shijiazhuang, is so huge, yet its name ends in *zhuang* – 'village'."

When the car reached a bend, a wild hare suddenly darted onto the highway. On hearing the blare of our horn, it bounded to a hollow in the escarpment to the right of the road. Its ears pricked, its tiny head twisted around and then the varmint returned to the asphalt again and scurried in front of our car. We accelerated and it doubled back and headed for the cliff face to the left. Like a downy knot of flesh, it somersaulted back from its target. Mu Tao then laughed at the speedy reflexes and quick-mindedness of the hare.

His topic soon shifted to tigers and he surmised: "A tiger is a tiger simply because it doesn't have the alertness of a hare. A tiger always crouches lazily as if it is dozing off. But once some prey appears, it pounces. After that, the big cat sprawls out quietly again, oblivious to anything around it."

I said that he was quite right, and when we got back, I would paint him a tiger.

"You have made this offer, so should honour it as a true gentleman."

I insisted that I was a gentleman when all was said and done. Mu Tao was happy and became talkative, praising the regal glamour of the tiger. Finally, he added: "The Chinese language is so precise. When we talk of tigers, we always call them 'old tigers' (*laohu*), as if to show our respect."

"Is that so? But we call mice 'old mice' (*laoshu*) as well!"

When we returned, sure enough I composed a tiger picture for him. However, once it was finished, I felt too fond of this portrait and refused to part with it. Mu Tao jeered at me, saying that I had painted a tiger, but with the narrow mind of a mouse.

"It's because I have the narrow mind of a mouse that I've decided to keep the tiger. Now I can be puffed up with the air of that noble beast."

II.

It was his way with language that first endeared Mu Tao to me. He has a pinched pair of eyes, which cast a coercive gaze. He talks in a halting way as if the words are being allowed to ferment multiple times in his stomach before being decanted drop-by-drop.

Mu Tao's main characteristic is his serenity.

The masses in our country are in a turbulent mood. And yet they are tired of articles that set out to incite. Many men of letters strive to surpass such knee-jerk anger. They square up to what seems eternal as well as the absence of true eternity before resolving to remain calm. Once that has been achieved, they can either write about the capriciousness of everyday life or learn from the example of calligraphers whose composure is feigned. Such people daub out words in a louche or haphazard fashion.

Writing articles is no different from the business of being a man. Just because you seek out a state of placidity, you are not guaranteed to attain it. A kind of anchoring force is required. This anchoring force is derived from the knowledge that there is a sublime realm. Mu Tao's articles bear some resemblance to the paintings of Huang Binhong (1865–1955). They survey and recast the national tradition from a global perspective. The dissemination and transmission of that tradition is what thus establishes an individual sense of value.

I remain somewhat in the dark about the circumstances of Mu Tao's birth and his life experiences – heaven only knows if he migrated from Arcadia or else the realm of devils. His serenity is inscrutable. Still, after reading and studying many of his articles I found that it is within his serenity that his wisdom and literary flair are manifested.

Mankind is evolving into those who are wise and those who are clever. Clever people are to be found everywhere, but they constantly inflict harm upon others, demeaning themselves into being petty men. Those who have wisdom are hard to find because they possess a special kind of artistic sense. They are apt to infer extraordinary things from the mundane. Everything can be expressed in three different ways. Mu, on the other hand, articulates his ideas with appropriate words and a correct attitude in an artful manner. Like a beautiful lady, the regions of plumpness and leanness are judiciously apportioned.

The literary field is a microcosm of society. Rascals and virtuous fellows are evenly distributed in every corner. Nowadays especially, it is hard to distinguish genius from tomfoolery. There are so many idlers and speculators. It is a pity that Mu Tao has not achieved great fame from writing. He has written sparingly. If we observe him quietly, it may be discerned that he is inured to short-term success. He has spent more time in meditation, collecting materials, reading various kinds of books, soaking up all the nourishment he requires. His mind is extremely vigorous.

These days, a group of young writers has emerged who appear more adept than the previous generation. This fills me with both respect and fear. I know that sometime in the future, he will produce his masterwork. I never expected that he would turn out a manuscript as long as his novel *The Original Sin*. Reading this book, and bringing to mind his narrow eyes, slow speech, and propensity to accrue power, I thought back to an old saying: "Heaven will curb the sharp-tongued; ghosts will conquer the proud."

Mu Tao came over to Xi'an from Shijiazhuang. Our relationship changed from author and editor to office colleagues and a feeling of ease imbued our work and daily lives. When we obtain fine tea, we entertain each other. When we have nothing to do, we read books randomly. Each man has his own smell, but perhaps those of a similar odour cleave together.

I have written a brief preface for what has turned out to be a substantial collection. It is rather like an obese man balancing a tiny hat on his head. The cap may be put on or left off. It may also serve as the introductory gong and drum, beating the overture to a theatrical performance.

Taking a Stroll in Chang'an City

I. AT THE FOOT OF THE CITY WALL

The building of the present city wall in Chang'an commenced in 1370 – three years after the founding of the Ming Dynasty. The edifice was completed in 1378, so it has been standing there for more than six centuries.

The ancient city wall has borne witness to countless events – human concord and contretemps, the fickleness of the world, justice and abuses, shifting clouds and floating dust as well as heavenly light and the shadows of the moon. All were imbibed by this spectator. At the summit of the wall, dynastic banners were unfurled and then lowered. The structure kept silent, refusing to pass comment. Whether in times of prestige or turmoil, it remained impassive. "Let it be." This may be the basic attitude of the old bastion towards the frenetic hordes inside and out.

Of all the sights in Chang'an City, the ancient wall elicits my greatest admiration and awe. Perverse phenomena cause a visceral reaction, but when ordinary artefacts last for ages, they assume the charisma of a deity.

Adjacent to the inside of the city wall there runs a narrow path named the "horse track". In ancient times it was frequented by peddlers and lackeys running errands. Nowadays it has contracted in width owing to the incursion of housing. In the morning and in the evening, stocky ladies squeeze along the path sideways.

A moat encircles the wall. The water is not deep, but it

is clear enough to shimmer. The silt at the bottom is dredged every few years, the last occasion being in 1998. The project was undertaken by military personnel stationed near Chang'an. Almost a whole regiment toiled away for the better part of a year. I recall that it started in early spring and was not finished by December. During the Spring Festival period, when citizens saw the ongoing slog on their TV sets, they were deeply moved and swarmed over to present tokens of appreciation. Some of them even joined in. During that season, silt-dredging became a hot topic in the city. According to the historical annals, this operation was carried out six times in the Qing Dynasty (1644–1912). In the Republic of China era (1912–49), when the so-called "New Life" movement was being advocated, the cleaning began once but was abandoned incomplete.

The banks of the moat have been planted with a perimeter park, eye-catching in its scenery, though multifunctional nevertheless. The section along the wall throngs in the evening, with lanterns swaying and lights jigging in time to the music. It forms its own half-covered, half-*alfresco* dance hall. Bands of Qin opera enthusiasts assemble to amuse themselves. Several strangers singing assorted roles spontaneously cluster into a troupe. Within days they will be firm friends.

The portion of park along the ring road appears more vigorous. Every daybreak before the road sweepers have arrived, folks have already descended here. This gathering contains even fewer spring chickens. Odd ones bring along a sword, but I have yet to see weapons of any other kind. The empty-handed may swing their hands, lift their legs to perform flexing exercises or bow deeply to loosen up the waist. A few even wave their arms in the posture of a shadow boxer. A while back, this would proceed to the strains of low, languid cassette music. Of late, the stereos have disappeared. The routines are better practised unaccompanied; the silence making the morning air crisper. In fact, the swordsmen seldom remove their blade from the sheath. When they reach the park, they select a spot and lay the weapon down before beginning their exercise of choice. Once they have sated their need, the sword is retrieved and they depart. Observing those scabbards scattered across the ground, one phrase crosses my mind, "peaceful restraint". By that I mean that the saber remains firmly encased.

Recently in the morning, another fascinating workout has appeared in the park. A few who practise morning exercises cut hair for others as a sideline, their swords replaced by implements such as razors and clippers bundled in a white cloth. Should a customer amble over, they are beckoned to squat on a stone stool, then the barbershop is ready for business. The price is down to the sitter's discretion. If nobody wants a trim, the hairdressers will swing their hands and legs or flex their waists in the meantime. The cold face of an idle tradesman is never to be worn.

Those who come here in the morning want to prolong their longevity. They all admit to being over-the-hill and no longer have any interest in material gain. Anyhow, these pastimes serve to encourage them. Zhou Zuoren (1885–1967) once stated: "Beyond our daily necessities, we must have a few diversions and frivolous entertainments. Only in this way can we cleave a meaningful existence." Looking at this from an alternative angle, if people's lives are merely saturated in joy and pleasure, then adversity can be taken as a dash of spice.

II. THE ZHONGNAN MOUNTAINS

The rainy season in Chang'an comes around in September. Fully fifteen overcast and wet days are to be expected then. According to historical accounts, nineteen days of torrential downpours is the record. The rain here is rather special since about half falls in the evening. The mornings see spells of drizzle. When the sun rises, the surface water begins to evaporate, so that although September in the city is rife with clouds and precipitation, the atmosphere is actually stiflingly humid. During the summer in the Tang Dynasty (618–907 AD), this was the period for "official vacations". That is to say, government officials at certain levels were given their leave. There were two reasons for this. One was the unbearable sultriness. The other was that the roads had become too muddy for smooth traffic.

The rain in Chang'an City has a peculiar characteristic. Showers usually begin in the south and migrate north or move from east to west. The southern portion of the city experiences the most plentiful annual rainfall, on average 1,000 millimetres. Lintong District in the east is the driest, receiving less than 600 millimetres per annum. There were scientific reasons behind the Emperor Qin Shihuang (247–210 BC) selecting this as the site for his mausoleum.

Ancient people were in the habit of touring the Zhongnan Mountains after the rain. This range is located 20 kilometres to the south of Chang'an City. The earliest reference to the Zhongnan Mountains is to be found in the *Tribute of Yu* section of the *Classic of History* (third or fourth century BC?). It states how: "The Rivers Qi and the Zhu were next led in a similar way (to the Wei), and the waters of the Feng found the same receptacle. Sacrifices were made to (the mountains) Jing and Qi. (Those of) Zhongnan and Dunwe (were also regulated), and (all the way) on to Niaoshu." The rivers and mountains mentioned in this book all lie within the territory of Shaanxi. The Qinling Range snakes from east to west reaching as far as Weiyuan in Gansu Province. In *The History of the Han Dynasty* (first century AD) it is recorded that: "The Zhongnan Mountains produce jade, gold, silver, copper, and iron, which provide raw materials for hundreds of craftsmen and furnish a livelihood for thousands upon thousands of citizens. Other fare includes non-glutinous rice, pears, chestnuts, white mulberries, hemp, and bamboo. The soil is suitable for cultivating edible canna lilies and the rivers are bursting with fish. The poor can garner a living here free from the spectre of hunger." Wang Wei (699–759 AD) wrote in his poem: "Looking back at the white clouds, the clouds appear blank." Li Bai (701–62 AD) reflected on how "when you go out to the southern mountain you will find infinite scenery".

The expression "Zhongnan mountain hermit" is now antiquated. It evokes how since ancient times scores of hermits chose to settle in this region. Back then, hermit referred to luminaries of talent who quested after solitude. Now, those who build villas in the foothills do not deserve this label. To begin with, they are not scholars. People who retire here do so for recreation and those who conduct business in these parts are mere merchants. What is more, they might yet prove the nemesis of this natural environment.

In recent years, much attention has been paid to environmental protection in Chang'an City. Standing atop the keep of the south gate of the city walls one can discern the outline of the Zhongnan Mountains in the distance. In the Ming Dynasty, there was a saying: "Sit and sip tea at the south gate, survey the beauty of Zhongnan." Today, when I ventured to the south gate, the mountain range were obscured and invisible. Perhaps a heavy smog was eclipsing them?

III. THE FISH IN THE LAKE

Outside my window reposes the so-called Lotus Lake; its name derived from the aquatic plants which grow in its shallows. In the summer, the water is carpeted with lush green leaves. In autumn, countless scarlet and yellow lotus blossoms reflect sun rays and moonbeams.

Among all the scenic spots in Chang'an, Lotus Lake undoubtedly warrants its title. Few foreign tourists know of its existence, making the lake somewhat like the private shrine of a grand family in the olden days. Only members of the clan can go there to worship and kneel before the altar. The lake is not huge, but it is situated in the centre of the old city, hidden several hundred paces away from the Drum Tower. The small lane leading to it is known as Lotus Lane and happens to be the shortest alley in the metropolis. Thirty walking strides are sufficient to reach its end. The street that passes by the lane is the broadest in Chang'an and called Lotus Road. All of the citizens who dwell hereabouts are residents of the Lotus District. This is the older part of the downtown area and is the most densely populated zone.

The clamour of the human world is cleansed away by the presence of the lake. It is as if there is an invisible barrier muffling the sound and fury of the society outside. My greatest wish has always been to live by the water. The current, however, should not be too fast-flowing and torrid. It seems my destiny to have encountered Lotus Lake. Every morning when I open my window, the lake senses that I am gazing at it and meditating.

Lotus Lake was originally the site of the Chengtian Gate, part of the Royal Palace in the Tang Dynasty. In 1378, during the Hongwu Period of the Ming Dynasty, the King of Qin, Zhu Shang, came to Chang'an. He set about laying out gardens and arboretums, diverting water from the Tongdi Canal to lower-lying regions and planting lotuses. Hence the creation of an eponymous pool. In 1635, in the eighth year of the Chongzhen Period, the place was renamed the "Happiest Garden". The reason behind this title was that "the King of Qin built this as a touring and banqueting hall. Here are ponds and flower gardens aplenty, which make this a choice venue for recreation. Access is restricted to nobles and men of fame." In 1668, the seventh year of the reign of the Emperor Kangxi of the Qing Dynasty, Governor Jia Han dredged the pool and changed its name to the "Releasing Creature Pool". As per the Buddhist custom of "mercifully loosing captive souls", fish were set free there to enjoy the pleasures of the open water. In 1922, in the eleventh year of the Republic of China Era, it was re-established as a park for ordinary visitors. From then on, the name Lotus Lake Park has been in common usage.

Although the title of the lake altered in accordance with the ferment of the world, the street alongside it has always been called Big Lotus Pool Street. The word "big" is obviously applied as an honourable epithet to the lake since no Small Lotus Pool exists in Chang'an. This street is, moreover, the hub of the Islamic community. An ancient mosque stands nearby. In the morning I am always awoken by the chanting of the Koran. The drone seems to emanate from the heavens but is actually an acoustic illusion. The sound echoes around one's ear cavities until it is headier and more intoxicating than blissful dreams.

The waters of Lotus Lake lack the enticing appearance and aroma of the Huaqing Hot Springs. Similarly, it is not infused with the bodily fragrance of the Concubine Yang (713–56 AD). Even so, its fragile ripples caress a man's heart. Most of the visitors to the lake are in the autumn of life. Very few could be counted as in their prime. Occasionally, lovers in the depths of ardour are to be seen, but these make a beeline for the bushes rather than enjoying the pool. They seek out the dense, gnarled shrubbery since branches that are tightly intertwined cannot be casually blown apart by the breeze. Under the soft moonlit night, couples embrace and exchange honeyed words on the wooden benches among the foliage. When they have nothing left to say, they kiss. When they are tired of kissing, they find other outlets.

Only the elderly are drawn here because of the lake itself. Whether covertly or overtly, amid the gusty, frosty, storm-swept and blizzard-filled conflicts between men, their hair blanches from black to white. Their energies dwindle and consequently they withdraw from the whirlpool of human desire. Some come along for idle pleasure, since life has been full of fatigue and they wish to set their minds at ease. Others seek to while away the time by angling. These people are surely belligerent by nature. They have tussled with the heavens, the earth and their fellow men. Their lifelong disposition towards violence has given way to a form of inertia. When people get old, their hearts, hands and feet are in want of employment, so they come here to fight with the fish.

So many aspects of human life, including youth, beauty, power, fortune and even the instinct to procreate, diminish over time. Each one is like a grain of sand slipping between your fingers. The trajectory from being in full possession of these qualities to being utterly denuded entails what is known as the "vicissitudes of life". The vicissitudes of life for each individual are graven on their face. No matter how sophisticated a person may be, these can never be concealed. A weathered visage is the book of the soul. Every last wrinkle is a concise hieroglyph. Age spots form the illustrations of this wondrous opus. Some well-phrased notes on the reversals of life are shocking to the eyes and heart. Chatting with an old man or watching some seniors converse from afar is like leaning over one's bed and cradling a book. With a twitch of the eyebrow one page is gone, with the flicker of a smile another is dispatched. As the old man turns around, the volume will slowly close.

Lotus Lake teems with fish. Standing on the bank, peering through the clear, crisp ripples, we can glimpse their slender forms or spot an outlier who prefers to cruise about alone. There are those who pair up, sweeping around in single file or fin-to-fin. Shoals pack together like disciples. When a human shadow is cast on the surface, they take flight in all directions with the haphazardness of arrows. In a flash, their tails whip up eddies.

I was quite familiar with one old angler. Every day, he planted two fishing rods in the same position. Every day, dozens of fish nipped at his bait. His rods were ever so delicate, capable of being extended or retracted as he saw fit. As bait he used dried flakes of meat and the remnants of leftover steamed buns. Whether crouching down or on his feet, his movements were dexterous. His every action from baiting the hook to casting the line and then winding it back were executed with the greatest panache. He was truly a dab hand at this. The old man slipped his catch into a porcelain jar by his side. There they would slither around at a rapid lick, trying to tolerate the stabbing pain in their mouths. When the jar was full, he would tip his haul back into the lake. Newcomers not blessed with great foresight promptly took the bait.

I ran into this fellow almost daily. Once we had grown more familiar, I praised his angling skills. He simply smiled in return and noted: "I am an old timer. I just need something to keep me amused." I don't know if there are any fish who, upon their release, intentionally return to be hooked for a second time. By the law of averages there must be some who will commit the same error twice. Fish have no developed memory.

In normal life what I dislike most of all is being made fun of. I had no idea how the released fish judged the old man. I supposed that if several of the bullied victims put their heads together there would surely be a barrage of cursing. "Damn it! You dare to hook me?" Just like a weakling being set upon by a strapping hooligan. After he or she broke free in a foul mood, teeth would be gritted and expletives let fly in an obscure place. "Your mother's *$#@! Pick on someone your own size!"

I hadn't seen that man for more than a month. At first, I thought that the cold weather was deterring him or maybe he had caught the sniffles and wanted to rest awhile. One day when I was really lost for anything to do, I dialled the landline number he gave me. The elderly woman's voice in the receiver knocked me for six. "He has passed away." On hearing no response from me, she asked: "Who are you?" I thought for a second and then explained: "I am one of his fishing chums." A heavy sigh was audible at the other end: "To start with, he was quite well. That day we were watching TV after dinner. Before the news was finished his head tilted against the armrest of the sofa. At first, I thought he had dozed off and didn't pay any attention. After a bit, when I patted him, his head felt cold. Hah! He was a worrywart all his life; never a single day's peace. When he retired, he died the moment he bowed down his head." For several days, the image of the old man keeled over the armrest flashed constantly in my mind. He was a fine looking fellow and dignified with it. His hair especially seemed to coruscate in waves in the breeze, giving the impression that from his youth until now not a single strand had ever been shed.

A few days later I visited the lake again. I thought there were bound to be more fish in his favourite spot than before. Free from the threat of perilous hooks, the fish must feel glad to be able to congregate there. When I arrived, I found that the water was preternaturally still and not a single scaly body was to be spied. I concluded they might have migrated to other places for the benefit of new traps.

People do not understand the joy of the fish. Maybe just like human beings, they choose to stay in hazardous zones. Or else they would be overcome with idle loneliness.

IV. CULTURE

The year of the horse is just around the corner.

The postage stamp designed to mark this year depicts a gaudily-pigmented clay figure modelled by the Hu family of Liuyin Village in Fengxiang County, Shaanxi Province. They have been famed for their craft for hundreds of years, producing two basic lines – the flat-backed wall plaque and the three-dimensional sculpture. The horse is only one of their forms, since other signature pieces include crouching tigers, tiger heads to be hung on the wall, rampant bulls, and effigies of the five vermin.

In June 1998, when President Clinton visited our city, Hu Xinmin, the custodian of the family craft draped a kaleidoscopically-painted raging bull around his neck.

This morning, Hu Xinmin's old friend Wang Yunkui called me. He told me that an exhibition of the Hu family's handiwork was to be held in Hong Kong during the Spring Festival. Hong Kong is a windswept and rainy city. I hope the porous clay Bodhisattva can serve as its own protector.

These days, Professors Chen Pingyuan and Xia Xiaohong, an academic couple from Peking University, are staying in Chang'an City. They are also delivering lectures on literature on TV. When I was reading the *Xi'an Evening Post*, I found that Professor Chen went to a secondary school to give an address. It is truly great that a renowned scholar should think to talk to adolescent pupils. This echoes the academic grace of the Republic of China era.

One major event in Chang'an City this month is that the prose magazine *Meiwen* will award 100,000 yuan to three secondary school pupils. The full title of the award is "The Golden Global Award for Elegant Teenage Prose". Mr Chen is one of the judges for the competition. Tongues will surely wag over whether it is proper to offer such a fortune to those of tender years.

V. GUESTS

Shortly after the Spring Festival, more and more people choose to share a New Year's greeting. Most of them use their cellphone. This newly-emerged rite is rather commendable. Sharing heartwarming platitudes over the phone avoids the foot-fatiguing chore of having to call around in person.

Today my cousin and his family came over from the countryside. They visit every year on the same day, bringing their "New Year's Consignment" from the land. The bulk of the package is edible, homegrown, handmade and brimming with flavour. In the past five or six years, they have favoured apples. My cousin is the owner of sprawling orchards, the repute of which is known far and near. He has new strains of fruit, capable of delivering bumper harvests and enviable sales.

When he crossed the threshold this time, his face was dark and I thought that perhaps his trade had slackened, leaving a surfeit of apples. After listening to him vent his grievances, I realised that, this year, apples are now cheaper than potatoes. The more he sold, the more revenue he lost. Still, he had to keep in business. I brought out the apples gifted by our work unit and let him estimate the price. He told me it would be considered fair if they fetched only twenty cents per kilo on the wholesale market. After he left, I went to the fruit and veg stall and observed that the highest grade apples were indeed only fifty cents per kilo – exactly the same amount as potatoes.

My cousin is rash-tempered. Usually he treats family members as per the maxim "daily beatings, constant cursing".

This time, his tempest had become a drizzle. His words to his wife were like a stroking breeze. As the apples had slumped in price, his temper had grown correspondingly better. Beholding his wife's contentment, couldn't this be considered one of the choicest pleasures in the world?

VI. RECORDS OF GREAT EVENTS

Meretricious things still have the capacity to move and touch people.

This month, a series of auspicious occurrences befell Chang'an City one after another. It was as if a sequence of set-piece dramas was being staged back to back. First, the National Confectionery and Victuallers Convention was held here. Overnight, one hundred thousand businessmen jammed into the city together with their merchandise. The big boulevards and small lanes were festooned with flags advertising sweets and alcohol. The next large commercial event was the East-West Trade Fair. Comparatively speaking, this exposition was better organised. At least no peddlers were hawking their goods on the streets.

During these two events, a number of celebrities visited to add glamour to the proceedings. They included Bora Milutinovic, the coach of the Chinese national football team, the famous pop singer Liu Huan, and dozens of others from film and television. Their appearance gratified the entertainment pages of all the newspapers in Chang'an.

On 5th April, thousands and thousands of Chinese from home and abroad flocked to worship the founder of their race, the Yellow Emperor. They held a lavish ceremony in front of his mausoleum and praised his spirit. Another great event was that the Buddhist relics of Sakayamuni were escorted out of the Famen Temple and taken to Taiwan, where they were worshipped. On the eve of departure, a grand Buddhist ceremony was orchestrated.

The most disgraceful thing this month in Chang'an was a football riot. A referee was punched and two police cars overturned. Dozens of hooligans were put behind bars. The Chang'an team was banned from playing home games. This was not merely a case of face being lost. Devoted local fans were left unable to watch a match live. One writer's words about Paris may be equally apposite to Chang'an: "This city may be a little recherché, but this is where its beauty resides. Its gains and losses also lie in its recherché nature."

VII. TWO MEN

The first man is a sot. During the National Confectionery and Victuallers Convention, he had two boxes of business cards printed and posed as the director of a wholesale division. These he doled out to stand after stand. His original intention was to sample fine spirits for free, but he never expected that a day or two before the end of the exposition he would receive telephone calls from dozens of distilleries eager to send his company products to preview. Helpless all of a sudden, he took out a short-term lease on a two-room office unit. Later, he claimed that the samples delivered in a three-day period were enough to last him a lifetime.

The second man is a friend of mine. He related an anecdote to me. One morning when he was passing the second ring road in a taxi, his vehicle came to a halt in a traffic jam. A boy of around ten was begging outside the car window. He took out two yuan. When the urchin had his money, he hurried to the next car.

In the evening, he encountered the same child outside a barbecue grill. A huddle of people were pawing and clouting him. A bystander said that he had been caught red-handed picking pockets. On hearing the plaintive howls of the youngster, my friend found the spectacle intolerable. After all, he was barely more than a lad of ten.

My friend pulled away the strangers who were mauling him and apologised for the boy's behaviour. The child wept and complained that he hadn't had a square meal in days. My friend took out a fifty yuan note and crammed it into his tiny soiled claw. He warned him not to steal things anymore. The boy escaped like a gust of wind before the weight of his words had sunk in.

After finishing his tale, my friend added that he knew that everything the little shit had said was claptrap, but could not explain why he still gave him some cash. My friend was not well-to-do. His actions spurred a moment of contemplation: people are willing to pay a higher price out of sympathy and pity than they are to ensure that virtue and ethics are upheld.

VIII. IRRATIONAL THINGS

There are two types of stroll which people do not care to take. One is alluded to by Thoreau, who maintained that "it requires a special dispensation from Heaven to become a walker". To be honest, in my heart I feel this type of stroll is deadly to mere mortals. It seduces people to meditate upon duties as lofty as the heavens. The second is strolling as exercise. There is no joy to be had from doing this. It is akin to business copywriting. Giving free rein to the imagination and opinions is forbidden.

Taking a stroll is actually an irrational thing. You step outside because your interest is piqued, and return when your heart is content. Only by this means can a stroll become interesting and splendid. Even if you stumble out aimlessly to escape the suffocating family atmosphere, you might find yourself spellbound by the dense willows and chromatic flowers. There is no rational basis behind these matters.

So many things in the world are irrational. For example, the division of time. When the world completes one circuit around the sun it is called a year. The moon orbiting the earth is called a month. The earth rotating one full revolution is known as a day. This kind of definition represents people's scientific understanding of the cosmos. Among all these divisions of time, we must also include the unit of the week. One week lasts seven days. Which celestial body orbits which other body to determine its length? There are minor fluctuations in the duration of a year, a month and a day. On the other hand, a week conforms to a precisely fixed time span.

Talking about the week, one surely broaches the topic of God. But where is He to be found? Among all these irrational things, great truth and rationality lie hidden waiting to be discovered.

Rational things all concur with the laws of nature. And yet this proves inadequate for the world of human beings. There must be something irrational added to the mix. Only in this way is the erudition of higher primates revealed. Nonetheless, when irrational things are determined according to strict rules, they become irrational. As time goes by, people take these rules for granted. Even though something defies rationality, it still has an active significance. For instance, monogamy, walking on the left-hand side of the pavement, and holding presidential elections every four years in the West.

In Chinese, the word "ethics" (*daode*) consists of two characters. One is *dao* ("way") which refers to the law of nature. The other is *de* ("virtue"), which is defined by strict rules or what we may call the "rules and regulations of man". *Dao* is, of course, of great importance to a dynasty. Who is willing to flout the laws of nature? Who is skilful enough to violate the laws of nature? When it comes to *de*, the subtlety emerges. From ancient times right up until the present day, the Chinese have stressed "virtuous governance" (*dezheng*). The periods when people crow loudest about virtue are actually when it is in short supply. It is just like in the vegetable market. The stallholders make the biggest din advertising what is rotting on the shelf.

Rules are the handles of the truth. Whoever can grasp those handles is truly a god. There is an old saying in Chang'an City which serves as an *aide de memoire*: "When your turn comes around, don't quibble with the rules."

Men's Mistakes

Up until the age of ten, my father was my role model. In my eyes he was both tall and mighty and so I imitated his manner of walking. In truth, his gait was rather ungainly. His knees would bend slightly as he went along and there was no musculature about his chest, leaving his belly noticeably protruding. I would even mimic the tone of his speech – as tranquil as the waters of a lake which barely fluctuate in temperature from one season to the next.

When I reached my ninth year, it dawned on me that he had gone off the rails. That summer my mother passed away. Only with great reluctance does the actual date ever pass my lips. That fact still presses down too grievously upon my heart. From then on, my father – a fit, middle-aged widower – began to drink with abandon.

Our home would only ever be peaceful when his neck was not flushed and his eyes were not bloodshot. Peaceful days of that kind were few and far between. After hitting the bottle, he would invariably doze off, his snoring pealing like a series of thunderclaps. Were he not to snore, it would be even worse. He would stamp his heels or hurl projectiles about the place. Every time this happened, my siblings and I would cower and watch on as the graceless drill ran its course. His erratic routines may have worked wonders for building up his pectoral muscles but only caused us anguish.

He has now been dead for more than ten years – the drunkard sprawled out one last time never to rise again. When I recall the past, what left the deepest impression are the days when my father's shortcomings were on full display.

I dislike men who garner your respect under duress. They sit behind an office desk and snort out their feelings through their nose rather than their mouth. This type of person usually likes to have a screen alongside them. Only a ghost can tell from what they are shielding themselves. Their eyelids droop without any reason and it appears as though they have landed from some celestial body superior to the Earth. In our hectic and disorganised lives, these petty officials who grant themselves airs are to be found everywhere we look.

Feeling self-satisfied is a general failing among all men. Sometimes this quality should be praised. At dusk when the breeze tickles the branches of the willow, most of the older husbands who promenade about the tree-lined avenue will adopt the same demeanour they once had when they accompanied their pregnant wives. They maintain a tangible distance from her as if they are noblemen in possession of some rare commodity. At this point, were the man to lift his tail and belt out a melody, nobody would raise an objection. Instead, the pride of the grandsire would prove infectious.

In striking contrast to women, men's flaws make them more appealing. Their faults can serve as a kind of lever, which renders them easier to govern. As for women, the opposite is true. The least shortcoming mars the whole surface, floating there perpetually like a stray blade of grass that refuses to sink.

One women's magazine featured a survey entitled: "What trait do you admire most in a man?" Among the thousands of responses they received, none mentioned "a serious and upright seating posture", "always speaking straight-faced" or "perfection in every area". Many women's attitudes are curious. It is as though they view this matter from the corner of their eyes. They like their man to "sprawl out on the bed and smoke", to "button their shirt up wrong again", to "appear mischievous when they grin", and to "remember my birthday two days late". The most intriguing letter came from an old dear in Chongqing. She could obviously flex her fountain pen with grace. Her note read: "This year I turned sixty-six. Our golden wedding anniversary is nigh and I am still waiting for my husband to put a foot wrong. He is three years my junior and all these years he has acted more obediently than our little grandson."

I have a classmate from university – a phenomenal fellow. Wherever he goes, he always stirs up a rollicking atmosphere. It is not what he says that is so significant, but whenever he opens his mouth everybody in his company will soon be beaming broadly – especially the womenfolk. Even some young female teachers are eager to discuss issues with him. His speech is pointed, humorous and bristles with empathy. Many women have grown fond of him. As an aside, he has no serious interest in courting them. Even so, the more he behaves like this the fonder the ladies become of him. This is bizarre.

In my university days, no girls showed any interest in me. Once, I deliberately opened my heart to a female classmate simply because I discovered that she was always looking at me. Hers was a stealthy glance, which as soon as others made it known that they were conscious of it, was soon discarded as a stratagem. Every time I saw her coming from afar, my heart would begin to pound. When she drew close, my eyes would move askance before my legs could be put into gear. As graduation approached, I resolved to invite her out on a date. I clenched my jaw and spewed a lot of illogical drivel. Other than my teeth, every part of my body turned to jelly. She listened attentively to my pronouncements and then declined on the pretence that: "We will soon be making our ways to separate ends of the Earth." When we parted, she commented: "Why is it that you lope along in that manner? To your credit, you have the air of a scholar. On the other hand, you walk like a woman who's lost her virtue."

Now when I bring to mind this episode, I realise that we were at that phase of "whoever loves me, I shall love them back". This experience taught me certain principles about how to become a man. Two years after graduation, when in half a stupor, I ran into a girl who I fancied. This was in a small florist's shop. Emboldened by the booze, I declared: "Go ahead and let me kiss you." She smiled among the masses of petals. Later, she became my lover. This sequence of events may sound a little astonishing, yet my venture did not go unrewarded. How can this be explained?

I think that if a man wants to quicken his pace, he must cast away the many encumbrances he bears on his shoulders and stomp ahead with a light heart and a light body. If you were to come across your sixty-year-old wife's testimonial of regret in the pages of a magazine, it would probably be too late. Perhaps the conclusion I have drawn is wrong, so my judgement should not be taken uncritically. Notwithstanding, I myself subscribe to this philosophy, and it helps me to attack my work with ever greater gusto.

Splendid Folk Customs

In my home village in the Huabei Plain we had a traditional custom. If a girl were to have the misfortune to die while still unmarried, her family would try every means possible to find a boy who had passed away in the same state. The two would then be buried together. No matter how hard the search proved, they were duty-bound to accomplish it.

Before the internment, the families would stage a wedding ceremony. In ancient times, wealthy families arranged extremely grand "ghost marriages". Even among ordinary folk, the two clans would unite for a "joyous toast". Many interpretations have been offered for this kind of union, but the most popular explanation goes like this. Should a teenage girl lose her life prematurely and not be granted a "ghost marriage" she had no chance of being reincarnated as a human in the next life. Although the spirit of the girl had done no harm to anybody, her heart would be engulfed by melancholy. In the night when the breeze was fresh and the moon high aloft, she would wail long and dolorously like an egret.

This is the stuff of legend. No one has in fact heard that sound in real life. A further possibility is that her family was so grief-stricken that it was a figment of their imagination. I believe that the phenomenon of the "ghost marriage" is absurd and defies all sense of reason. The only potential benefit is that it may provide a crumb of consolation for the wounded heart of the household.

When I was in secondary school, the Four Clean Ups Movement happened to be in full swing. So many authentic traditional customs were being arbitrarily swept away. Pernicious practices, like the "ghost marriage", were bound to be targeted too. Nevertheless, one tragedy that occurred at that time convinced me that there was a splendid facet behind the perniciousness.

In the spring of that particular year, the winds and rains appeared in good time and the climate was benevolent to both men and crops. Few people showed any marked concern about how the land was being cultivated. The heavens, however, lent their assistance. When summer came around, the crops seemed to become the delinquent offspring of the villagers. Lacking parental governance, they shot up in a frenzy. My home village lay in a cotton-growing district. Field after field of waist-high cotton plants cloaked the land like the cells of a honeycomb. One huge patch fused into the next. Even those with the keenest eyesight could not detect where they came to an end.

It was at this critical juncture that a bollworm epidemic struck the country. The bollworm is a kind of nocturnal insect. Somewhat in the manner of bats, they like to advance in swarms. Their tiny wings are brown or dark-shaded, polka-dotted with a black picotee along their edges. People find their appearance disconcerting. Most creatures are adorable in their infant stage. The bollworm is an exception. Even their pupae are revolting to behold. The olive-hued, fleshy, elongated strips which constitute their bodies loll about on the cotton branches. Still they display an appetite as voracious as a silkworm. Cotton fields which bear the brunt of the onslaught will be reduced to a forest of twigs in barely a week or ten days.

The plague elicited the same reaction as a wildfire. Everyone, whether male or female, young or old, must set to work combatting the inferno. All of the students in my school also trooped out *en masse* to help the farmers.

The method of eradicating the bollworms involved us combing the area like a dragnet. Together we doused the crops with pesticide. Our class was given four sprayers with the canisters to be strapped to our backs. In actual fact, the canisters were little more than crude plastic boxes. One would operate the stirrup pump with the left hand and direct the nozzle with the right. As we were in Year Ten we were given a lighter workload, the quota being to spray sixty *mu* of fields in one day. I remember how we would reach our "target fields" ten *li* away from our school before daybreak. I was given the technician's job, being responsible for diluting the chemical solution. The sprayers had to be filled with the exact proportions of water and pesticide. The chemical we used in those days was marketed as Joyful Fruits. It was a kind of organo-phosphate that caused death by inhalation. This oily, milk-like substance was noxious. An elderly local farmer told us that the smell might be vile, but it was not toxic to human beings. The experience of that day exposed the error of his words.

Soon after midday, two of my classmates felt nauseous and suffered headaches. In the evening, eight people from our school, including the physics teacher, were admitted to hospital. The next morning the grave news reached us. A female student from the sixth form had died in spite of every attempt being made to save her. Her surname was Wang and she was very timid and bashful by nature. She would even bow her head in embarrassment when she smiled. As a representative of my class, I went to pass our condolences onto her family. I will never forget how her mother seemed ready to die from grief. Several people tried to carry her off, though her body sprawled on the ground, half-paralysed. Her hands clawed at the air and her mouth was agape. No cry was audible. That morning a sixteen-year-old flower had left us for good.

The schoolmaster was an army veteran. All year round his face was stony serious and whatever the season he favoured military footwear. In the winter, he wore shoes with ample toe-space and in the summer plastic-trimmed plimsolls. Despite trying to give him a wide berth in winter, plenty of male students were dealt a kick up the rear. After that sad morning, the schoolmaster disappeared for a fortnight. At last he returned from Tongxiang District in Beijing, 200 *li* away. He brought with him the corpse of a teenage boy who had perished in a motor accident. He buried him together with our deceased schoolmate Wang. Not long after that he was removed from his post and it was purported that he had been incarcerated on the grounds of spreading "feudal" ideology in our community.

It is many years since I left my hometown. The original county town has been subsumed by urban sprawl. Even the name of the county has been erased from the map. Once, when I was walking along the streets with my former classmates, we brought to mind the old spectacle of endless cotton fields and sighed over the sweeping changes. A classmate of mine got the worst thrashing from the schoolmaster. Following his removal from his position, the big-shoed teacher left the education system. His own learning had been piecemeal and he studied only as far as elementary school. He subsequently became a security guard for a private firm and then retired. The "joint burial" incident caused him to win favour with all the children in our school.

My former classmate and I went to visit him at home. By this time, he had been felled by a stroke and his eyes were lifeless. He could not even recognise who was who.

We both offered a deep bow at the foot of his bed.

Fine Pink Hands

I have nothing to my name save for a contented household, with a placid, kindhearted wife and a clever, delightful daughter. Every time I open the door and enter our home, the tangible aura of the "family" engulfs me from head to toe. This is my good fortune! I have the satisfied sense of possessing everything worthwhile in the world.

Life itself is indeed interesting. Unfortunately, there are those who do not approach it in an interesting way. Take, for example, emotions. Emotions are the lifelong root of a man, but these only become a source of beauty and trigger affection when they are genuine. A man comes into the world bawling and cavorts about in the dust for dozens of years before returning to the other realm. The only thing he can take away with him are emotions. As for other matters, not even emperors and kings are able to keep hold of them. Faced with this futility, they engrave their sentiments onto stone tablets that some future generation might crush into smithereens.

In life, Chairman Mao augured great and magnificent achievements. Few mortals past or present can be compared with him. The loneliness of his later years was also unrivalled. He devoted his entire being to his motherland. Still, from middle age he chose a turbulent wife with whom to live out his days. In his last few remaining years, he could not even savour the consolations of a family life as ordinary folk do. This is indeed a tragedy.

Emotions form the everlasting truth. The house in which

people reside may feel firm and sturdy, though it can still be torn down at any time. You can touch the furniture which keeps you company day and night, but this can be replaced once it becomes shabby and tumbledown. The clothes worn in all four seasons will fade someday. The parents who gave you life will eventually bid *adieu* to this world. Even your skin will wrinkle and age, your eyes blur, your ears fall deaf, your teeth drop out, and your virility attenuate into nothing. Only the true emotions in the depth of your heart remain completely devoted to you. They accumulate and form a thicker sediment and become more dependable by the day. A monk shaves his scalp bald to shake off the emotions which filled his head with fire. A person devoid of emotions can possess nothing that is true. Only through this route can those brethren achieve the state known as "emptiness" (*kong*) in Buddhism.

Emotions are the most difficult matter to enunciate clearly. For instance, a devoted husband and wife might appear to have been fused together with epoxy resin. Their emotions are transparent and strong. Once parted, though, all these properties are reduced to nothing, like a deflated balloon. Everything they formerly possessed evaporates like fog. What is left behind is even more frigid than water in winter. Hence, when a person becomes capable of narrating the course of his affections in nuance and detail, explaining them in dispassionate language, it denotes that this stage of his emotional life is drawing to an end.

Emotions are the most commonplace of things as well. There is no distinction between so-called "great love" and "humble love". It all depends on the different characters of those involved. A great man is propelled to greatness because of his achievements and personality, not owing to how sweetly he can love. The love a housewife brings to a family may be more professional in nature since she has no other objects to distract her mind. In fact, just as you eat at mealtimes and drink at teatime, you should go and love when you have somebody to love. Emotions are the physical and lifelong necessity for human beings. There is no other noble need. A man who is captive to his emotions has no regard for food and tea. A man may also behave like a hungry ghost – an unquiet spirit back from the dead desperate to sate some carnal or gustatory need. He too is unable to share normal, healthy love.

Ancient men of letters cherished a most exalted state of mind, namely "reading a book at night with a red-sleeved maiden adding fragrance". Mr Liang Shiqiu (1903–87) commented that this mindset was not so propitious. When a man happened to be perusing a book in the coolness of the night, if a pair of pink hands should sway from left to right in front of him, he would become distracted and no longer focus on the text. To be precise, this clause is a reference to an idle heart and mind. The volumes he read were not the Classics required as revision for the Imperial Examinations – a case of polishing the gun in preparation for promotion.

Chinese men of letters paid attention to idle leisure, being carefree and lazy in temperament. Scholars were particularly notorious for being sluggish. Besides indulging themselves by journeying through mountains and waterways, those who had attained literary eminence were fond of reclining on their side on the bed and dipping into multifarious volumes. That is why ancient Chinese texts were printed with the type running vertically. The soft texture of the paper made them easy to bind together with thread. The writing was read from left to right so the pages could be rolled up as the eyes scanned them. Western books designed with leather bindings and stiff paper are properly read before a desk in an upright, solemn posture. If you read them lying down, the task of lifting requires some muscular exertion and there is the ever-present danger of serious injury should the book slip and strike you on the head.

After the scholar had supped his fill of tea, he would slump down on the bed and leaf through his favourite volumes while the fragrance of his beloved muse percolated through the air. From time to time, a pair of hands accustomed to embroidery kneaded his waist and legs. This state of mind surpasses words. The "fragrance" in the air was more a kind of emotion, originating from an innocent heart and culminating in a relaxed brain.

"Fine pink hands", three words that appear in a poem by Lu You (1125–1210), are also believed to derive from this kind of mood. What is fine is not the hands, but the heart.

Several days ago, I went to dine in a restaurant in Beijing. The premises were handsomely decorated without being roomy. All the tables and chairs were varnished in ancient-style black lacquer. Sitting in a corner listening to the traditional Chinese stringed music, trilling from a laser disk, I was overcome with the sense that I had become an ancient man of letters. The names on the menu were ancient and elegant as well. There were no vulgar names like "fish-flavoured pork strips" or "fried tofu with green onion". Each had a title borrowed from ancient poetry. The only regrettable thing is that customers couldn't deduce what they were ordering and so didn't know what they would end up eating.

I ruminated for a long time and then ordered one dish:

fine pink hands. After choosing it, I asked the waitress if it was a kind of dessert. She smiled and went away with a swish of her hips. Very soon, she came back carrying a plate bearing a pig's trotter sliced in half. This dish is surely very easy to cook, although it needs a chef of calibre to prepare it to gourmet standard. First it should be braised until brown and then pared in two with a cleaver. The finishing touch is a basting of boiling oil.

While eating, I sighed deeply, thinking about this new interpretation of love. The restaurant is located in the alley closest to Tianmen Street. If you walk along the street for fifty metres and then turn left, you will spot it.

Bunny Love

Bunny was greedy. His manner of eating was ungainly. Vegetable leaves would be chewed with a tad more grace as though he were a poor scholar dining at his father-in-law's home, feigning good deportment despite being starving in his belly. The effort of gnawing at a raw carrot revealed how his lips were cleft.

Bunny's mouth was naturally misshapen. All too aware of this, he seldom broke into a squeak. When somebody grabbed him by the ears, the most he would do was to scratch and paddle with his paws and legs. If pinched too hard, a few screeches would signal his pain. The stupidity of a pig is shown by its tendency to squeal at the lightest of pats. Bunny knew the rule well – it is best if clumsiness remains hidden. In contrast, people who stammer, have oversized tongues and the harelipped are apt to be voluble. This makes others feel awkward and concerned.

Bunny took refuge in lapin slyness. As cunning specimens of his kind are said to have three dens, this is quite understandable. After all, the weak require a sanctuary and room for retreat. There is no need for the mighty to have multiple hideouts. Wherever a tiger roams automatically becomes its domain.

I was born in the Year of the Rabbit, as was my wife. We have shared the same den for a number of years and have never quarrelled. It is not that we suppress our anger. Instead, we are too languid to start an altercation. Should one of us run into something upsetting outside, once we return home we gently let it off our chest. My wife is a design editor. Most of the time, the bunnies she draws mimic our own demeanour and spirit. My young daughter is not yet skilled at writing with a pen, but she loves to sketch bunnies too. Hers are wild ones which bounce and bump around; far from the serene images my wife can conjure up.

Last year, my wife bought a pair of albino rabbits. They were only one month old and shuffled along the floor as if they were still unsure how to employ their legs properly. We found a large cardboard box to serve as their new home. The flap had to be pushed inwards from the outside so they could not escape.

My daughter took charge of feeding them. She grew quite fond of having the responsibility. She declared: "My pa and ma cook meals for me, so I will cook for them." She then went to the kitchen and scrabbled about for carrots. I told her that the bunnies were too young to be able to munch away at root vegetables. "Do they have toothache? We shouldn't give them toothache. That really hurts." My daughter is keen on sweet foods, so she knows only too well this agony. With those words, she reached for some greens to rinse. I then repeated: "Bunnies cannot eat veggie leaves washed in water. If they do, they will get ill. If they get ill, they may die."

This left her stunned for a while. She then said: "Why do I eat washed greens?"

I explained: "You are not a little bunny and you weren't born in the Year of the Rabbit."

"You and Mummy were born in the Year of the Rabbit, but you eat washed greens as well," she replied in an earnest tone.

"We are human beings. If we eat things without washing them, we will get poorly. Bunnies are not people. They get poorly after eating washed things."

Once she had comprehended that there was a distinction between us and rabbits, she began to draw bunnies chomping away at green grass or green vegetables. In order to confirm that their food was *au naturel* she deliberately flicked some spots of ink to represent dirt.

Such joyous days lasted barely two months before trouble loomed around the corner. First of all, we could not sleep for the sound of the bunnies scratching away at the cardboard at night. Listening to the squelch of them eating became increasingly unbearable, as if a talon were prodding away at one's heart. In the daytime they would patter around the skirting boards, their dubious behaviour curiously rat-like. Later on, we sensed that the she-bunny's belly was growing swollen in a manner not explained by over-eating. Then, it dawned on us that they were in fact a buck and doe and had been pleasuring themselves in the box. The rice was already cooked, so to speak.

When we were buying the animals, we feared that a solitary one would be tortured by loneliness. To make their lives easier, we purchased two of them. We never anticipated that they would reach maturity so soon. My neighbours told us that before the female gives birth she will burrow a warren for herself. The pit would be very deep with curving tunnels, shielding the scene of labour from human eyes. She would only bring the whole litter to the surface when the babies were fully mobile.

Our narrow apartment couldn't handle the bunnies' attempts at digging. Also, the doe might worry herself feverish over the impenetrable concrete floor. Mulling over this repeatedly, we resolved to send them to relatives in the countryside. On the day of the bunnies' departure, I drank a glass of liquor before them, announcing: "Please take this as a belated toast on your nuptials."

When our relations removed the rabbits, we concealed the matter from our daughter. We sent her to play in a neighbour's home. On her return, she saw they had gone and urgently asked me their whereabouts. I told her truthfully: "Mrs Bunny had babies in her tummy. We moved her to the hospital to let them come out." I knew she was afraid of going to the hospital. She wept on hearing this and took on a pitiful appearance. Still, she dare not mention the word "hospital".

After that, she was intent on pushing us further on the issue and each time we fobbed her off in the same way until she was tearful. One day without thinking my wife said: "We don't know how big the litter was." My daughter interjected: "How could the little babies get into the mummy's tummy?" I answered that she had swallowed them one by one.

Over the following few days, my daughter refused to eat green vegetables. Every time, we racked our brains over how to persuade her. It was futile. That was until one day I looked at her with wide eyes and asked her the reason why. She timidly opened her mouth: "I am afraid that I'll get baby bunnies inside me and then I'll have to go to the hospital." My daughter's complexion altered once she mentioned the hospital.

The business of the bunnies was somewhat like a husband and wife in ancient times. Under the will of the heavens, a go-between would place a female and a male stranger together and then the two would follow the flow of the river for the rest of their lives. When they had a burgeoning brood of children, their feelings would appear white and plain like the callouses on their palms. Sometimes, they might experience a numb sensation, but there would always be a direct link to their hearts. If you sliced into them, it would hurt.

An Era without Nursery Rhymes

Mr Dong Qiao has penned a short article entitled "An Era without Nursery Rhymes". The 1,000-word piece of prose describes two children. One is a Polish girl who survived the Nazi concentration camps of World War II. The other lives in the present-day – a ten-year-old American boy who has lost his father and longs to fly over to visit his relatives. What Dong Qiao wished to convey is that young souls mature rapidly in the face of dire hardship.

Mr Dong Qiao resides in Hong Kong and his articles always incorporate materials from abroad. If he lived in a city in Mainland China, such as Xi'an, this essay would have a different slant. Nowadays, children barely have a childhood at all, let alone one without nursery rhymes. When a foetus has just assumed its primitive shape in the womb, the vibrations of musical notes begin to be felt from outside, initiating its prenatal education.

After the birth, the parents will only break into broad smiles if the infant grabs a pen or a book in the "Foretelling the Child's Future Vocation" ritual. At the age of two, he or she is asked to digest the *One Thousand Character Primer* and, at three, recite the *One Hundred Family Names*. Parents who insist on this are those familiar with traditional Chinese learning. Couples who do not have such a background just force the child to recite whatever they can lay their hands on.

Last night on television, a four year old was shown skilfully declaiming from memory dozens of Tang Dynasty poems. The host then called on all the honoured studio guests to applaud. Tang Dynasty poetry is like high grade tea with a fulsome flavour. A child of this age is not a worthy receptacle. He or she should sip milk.

When children enter primary school, it is as though a nail is being driven into a wall and it cannot extricate itself through its own energies. In the reception class, they compete over who can memorise Chinese words written in pinyin and who can best recite their times tables. In Class Three, they bury their heads in the Maths Olympiad. By Class Four, they have started after-school English classes. As soon as they enter the sixth year, they, like their parents, have fretted themselves into a daze over how they might gain admission to a superior middle school. Middle school is even more fiercely competitive, the screws having been twisted tighter. Every day they shoulder a kilos-heavy hod of teaching materials and supplementary literature. My neighbour's child has just sat the college entrance examination and been accepted by Peking University on account of his formidable results. I asked him how he felt about middle school. His answer made me shudder with fear: "For the sun to rise, the nightmare must run its course."

I am still young, but my ideas are old fashioned. I maintain that children should be allowed to be children. Come what may, it is necessary to retain some childhood interests. If the present situation in schools persists, how will they recall their tender years when they are old? Maybe they will only remember computer games or how they spent whole nights in the internet cafe?

Youngsters today really do not have any nursery rhymes to call their own. For those who do, they are just a few clichéd foreign fairy tales. Contemporary Chinese authors are not prepared to write for children because they deem it a less serious form of literature, too facile and unlikely to capture mainstream attention. No wonder when middle school students tackle creative writing, all they come up with is bundles of clouds and mist, disconnected from any concrete reality.

    A few days ago, I travelled deep into the Qinling Mountains and brought back specimens of butterflies belonging to various species. When my daughter saw them, she became besotted with the insects and could not bring herself to let them go. How drab such a childhood must be! When I was a kid the words of the nursery rhyme still rang true and *butterflies fluttered by everywhere.*

Knocking a Wooden Fish

When a monk recites his *sutras* he strikes the wooden effigy of a fish with a baton. What has the fish done wrong? It is beaten in the Grand Hall of the monastery.

I guess this is because it lacks a thinking mind and brains. A real fish does possess a mind, together with a smattering of brain cells, but never uses them. Applying its mere dram of wisdom, it jumped into the sea and swam, not having a clue about how vast and deep the waters were.

When a man is in his infancy, he kicks his legs around blindly. They are always raised up high and plash here and there. When he learns to walk, his limbs gradually become steady. Human legs carry the weight of human life and so rheumatism in that region is a bane borne out of tribulation. Upon reaching middle age, he comes home after a busy day and his legs feel as though they are lined with lead. Only a good relax can enable him to sleep soundly. A man starts to age from the legs upwards. When he can no longer walk, it means that his life has almost come to an end.

The road is arduous. In other words, the course of life is never smooth. The legs are troublesome, but the heart even more so.

One year when I returned to my hometown, my younger brother piped up: "You are a colleague of the famous writer Mr Jia. Would you please get him to write a piece of his calligraphy showing the characters 'Hard to become muddled'?" I asked him why he wanted these characters. He told me that his colleagues, who had different ideas to him, were always causing strife. "This is because you are muddled," I reflected. "How can you become even more muddled? Let me write four characters for you – 'Be a sensible person'."

He then said: "Just write these three words for me – 'with ordinary heart'."

"Are you not ordinary enough? What you lack is the heart to move upwards. Use your brain and try to progress. Earn more money and support your wife and kids – these are the most important things."

My younger brother listened to me. Later, he managed to remain on civil terms with his colleague. His income gradually became healthier and his children went on to study at a key secondary school. "Hard to become muddled" and "with ordinary heart" are lessons to be learned after one becomes really broadminded in life. When one is tolerant and open-minded it is "hard to become muddled". Having an even temper is synonymous with having an ordinary heart. If a person has failed his primary examination, there is no practical use in him trying to enroll on a post-doctoral programme. Even if he is able to answer the questions, the answers must be cribbed from someone else.

Worshipping the Buddha is "asking for help from a higher authority". It is a spiritual enquiry. The ordinary people are sympathetic. When the government cannot or is unwilling to solve some headaches, they have to go to the Buddha for help; for instance, when they want to have a baby son, when their kids want to go to university, when they want to find a job, when they want to have a peaceful household, or when they are suffering from various mystery ailments.

The Buddha is the great authority. When people confess

their problems to him, even if they cannot be solved, they may feel a sense of solace in their heart. That is why the temples becoming more and more prosperous every day. The greatness of the Buddha lies in that he listens conscientiously to and draws himself closer to the bitter cries of the masses.

The government should implement a policy that bans civil servants from asking for help from a higher authority at the temple. This should be upheld using auxiliary methods of enforcement. People should stop them half-way along the road. Let his higher authority lead his people back. If there are troublemakers, place a tape recorder in front of the Buddha. This will record the voices of the government civil servants whose heartfelt "wish" to hug the foot of the Buddha is exposed. Should this event be replayed, it would be vividly compelling. There are bound to be some inside stories and shady dealings.

When someone draws near to the Buddha with a burdened mind, they are not truly worshipping him. Their worship is conditional. When their requests are not fulfilled, they will besmirch the Buddha. Allowing one's heart to draw near to the Buddha constitutes genuine worship. We should approach him with a sincere heart, fully prepared to do his bidding whether large or small. Only then will he feel the leisure to deliver more living creatures from torment.

Culture has Blood and Flesh

Culture is alive; or, in other words, culture only endures if it possesses a life force. Liang Shuming (1893–1988) once wrote that "culture is everything upon which our lives depend".

How are we to interpret this sentence?

Eating represents the culture of food, behind which there is agriculture. Dressing up represents the culture of clothing, behind which there lies industry. Behind eating and dressing up there is the culture of commerce. Whatever is popular is labelled "fashionable culture". Whatever is outdated is labelled "backward culture". Housing represents the culture of architecture. Travel represents the culture of transportation. In peaceful times, the culture of leisure reigns. Wartime gives rise to martial culture. Birth, ageing, growing sick, and death concern the culture of social customs. The cultivation of a man is dependent upon education. The development of a country is reliant upon science and technology. To be endowed with knowledge of all historical facts, including one's ancestors is to be rooted in traditional culture. The real greatness of a nation in a forest of world cultures is revealed by its openness to, and willingness to absorb, foreign culture.

The manner in which a man conducts his business forms his character, that is to say his personality. Once the manner in which a group of people in a particular region conduct their business accumulates collectively, like sediment, then it becomes known as a "culture".

In China, the differences between collectives, with their

own characteristics, are both distinct and concrete. Those who live along the Yellow River and those who live along the Yangtze River exhibit marked differences in their diet, clothing, shelter and transportation. Along the Yellow River, the people of Shaanxi, Gansu and Shanxi are close neighbours. The people of Henan and Shandong live adjacently. The people of Qinghai and the people of Ningxia dwell shoulder-to-shoulder. Yet, even among these groups the variation in their collective characteristics is quite obvious. Along the Yangtze River, there are striking divergences between residents of Hunan and Hubei, those of Jiangsu and Zhejiang, and the Shanghainese. If we set our sights more broadly, the differences between the people of Beijing and those of Guangdong are even more striking.

As far as Shaanxi Province is concerned, there are great contrasts between the people of Guanzhong, those of southern Shaanxi, and those of northern Shaanxi. In the Guanzhong Plain there are differences between the people of the west and the people of the east. In northern Shaanxi, the people of Yan'an and the people of Yulin are distinct. In the southern Shaanxi, Shangluo people, Hanzhong people and Ankang people are scarcely of a piece. There are two old sayings concerned with cultural personality. One is: "Customs vary every ten *li*. A particular land nurtures particular people." The discrepancies between folk customs and social customs are slight. Another saying goes: "Grow up by drinking from the same river." We may occupy opposite banks, but share the same water. When we study regional culture, we not only look for diversity, but also seek mutual interactions and the power of combining these together.

The cultural personality of a region is the specific image of a region. The carefulness of the Shanghainese, the directness and openness of the people of the northeast, and all that is muttered about those from Henan. These are like an indelibly marked brand. Cultural construction is the construction of a regional image. This image could not be achieved in a day or two through "more, faster, better, and cheaper" means. It also does not mean that when there is money there is fortune and, as a result, that the cultural image becomes greater and more glorious. Nowadays, the economy of China is the "second greatest" in the world, but the integral image of our behaviour in the eyes of foreigners does not, to be honest, warrant this ranking. Can we even qualify for the top twenty?

In this aspect, surely modern Chinese people should feel a sense of remorse towards their ancestors. Their ancestors are losing face. China is labelled as the "Country of Rites". There is an established standard of conduct for every station of life. "Benevolence, righteousness, propriety, wisdom, and sincerity" are inherent in the hearts of everyone. Now there are two popular phrases for self-criticism: "lacking sincerity" and "lacking belief". Actually, these have not been properly stated. What is lacking is a benchmark. We do a lot of things now that are not according to the norms established by our ancestors.

The present administration emphasises in a high tone the "prosperity of culture", but I think first things first. We should have a clear understanding of what culture is.

Civilised People

In a surprisingly remote land, the grass grew densely and vigorously. Fragrant flowers were in full bloom, rocks and stones of various formations stood inanimate, and water rippled, shimmering with light. Soaring birds and charging animals became enmeshed in the same food chain. These carnivores were neighbours as well as predators.

One day, two capable folk – a man and a woman – came along. No one knew why they chose this place or for what purpose. The fact is that when they arrived, they felled the trees and built the first ever house here. The pair mowed grass to generate the first kitchen smoke. In order to survive, they had to adapt to the region. One year later, their child was born.

Gradually, other travellers began to settle hereabouts. The kids grew up. Many years later both the population and the smoke had mushroomed. Some wary wild animals were domesticated and became household livestock. Other more headstrong beasts fled afar from man's weapons and the heat of the flames. The population burgeoned. Grass, bushes and forests were torched and the bounds of the vegetation receded rapidly. Streets unfurled between residences, criss-crossing and bisecting one another. Then schools, shops, post offices, banks, outdoor markets, trading mansions, and administrative blocks materialised. Not until this point did they name the piece of land the "city".

It thus became the standard view that those who lived in the city were civilised people. However, years later, the urban population had increased yet further. High-rises had replaced single-storey buildings, jutting relentlessly into the skies. Mules and horses had been superseded by automobiles, with the city dilating to an unprecedented scale. People's survival skills had become more acute. At this stage, the expression "environmental pollution" entered the vocabulary. In the face of their own turbulence and unease, and being vexed by a plethora of infectious diseases, folks began to yearn for the original primeval landscape.

On weekends and red letter days, they would head for the mountains and meadows for recreation. What is more, they sowed flowers at home and planted saplings out front. Architects designed floral traffic islands to plug the teeming crossroads and turfed over both sides of the street. They even invented the bespoke rooftop garden to perch at the summit of the tallest skyscrapers.

In an effort to unsully their consciences, the *nouveau riche* entrepreneurs sought out the unreached tribes of Africa and South America. They spent a fortune purchasing the very same soaring birds and charging animals their predecessors had driven away and placed these specimens in the municipal zoo. Fences penned off the captive creatures from visiting children. One day, someone slaughtered a wild swan with a high-tech rifle. All the newspaper readers and TV viewers in the city cursed the miscreant in unison. "Barbarian! So uncivilised!"

Civilisation almost always leads us as the vanguard. Nevertheless, it sometimes creeps up on us like a mother standing at the front door calling out earnestly and anxiously. Dusk has fallen and her kids haven't returned home yet.

The Servers within the Organs of the Human Body

The brain receives notification from the organs of the human body.

When one is hungry one eats; when one is thirsty one drinks; when it is cold one puts on extra clothes; when one is sleepy one searches for a pillow; when a person's back aches he massages his waist; when a person's leg is numb he wallops it with a fist; when one feels wronged and depressed one takes a walk to lighten the heart. When the proper time comes, one attends primary school, high school and then university, striving for an MA and a PhD. This is the modern equivalent to succeeding in the ancient imperial examinations. In the fashionable modern world it is known as "reading to bring about the rise of the People's Republic of China". As more time passes, one ties the knot, enjoys the lucent candles of the matrimonial chamber, and falls about in a disorderly scramble like the clouds on high. The conjugal obligation is thus fulfilled. All of these matters form the daily routine of the brain.

When one sees delicious food, one eats a little more. When one runs into an alluring person, one wants to do a double-take. When sweet words enter the ears, one wants to listen further. This is human nature. Even so, there should be boundaries that are not transgressed. People aspire to a higher position. As a sesame plant blossoms, it grows loftier and loftier. Our adversaries become more rotten day by day and we constantly improve. All of these are meant as words of encouragement. If one wants to follow these blueprints one must first have clarity in the brain and overcome all giddiness. One should be aware of the dangerous dimension behind these words. When one does something foolish, in the Xi'an dialect we call it "having water on the brain" (*naozi jin shui*). Embezzlers, thieves, rapists and murderers not only have water on the brain, their grey matter is truly flooded.

There are two entities hidden in the human belly: knowledge and what we have eaten. These two things are different in nature yet conform to the same principle of circulation. All have been consumed in a certain form or shape under the guidance of the brain. Boiled dumplings, noodles, rice, meat, and vegetables are food. Textbooks, novels, classic works, and the deeds of those who set a good example constitute knowledge. They are digested and converted into energy, which is distributed throughout the organs of the body. That which cannot be digested is expelled through certain outlets. If a person eats "pearls of literary Chinese" and then expels them wholesale as "pearls of literary Chinese" it means that they have not been digested properly. Studying is the same as eating. It is not a case of the more the better. As long as one is full that is enough. When one has eaten one's fill, somebody must return to work. That is the purpose of eating. If one has a bellyful of books and is possessed of learning and ability but makes nothing out of it, one is just a bucket for food.

Tying their hair to a rafter and digging a bodkin into their buttocks were two measures by which scholars in ancient times forced themselves to read attentively. These means of self-mortification prevented them from falling asleep. In modern society, these methods are almost unheard of. What is more commonly reported are case of failure, where people have sought unsuccessfully to have their eyes surgically enhanced or their noses lifted or their faces and waists made more slender. No matter whether the object is study or beauty, none of these procedures should be advocated. The best recourse is to elevate one's thoughts to such a degree that trouble is not brought upon one's own body.

Master Zhuangzi (late 4th century BC) once described three disabled people. They were Wang Tai, Shen Tujia, and Ai Taita. The first two had no shins, so they were known as the "footless ones". The last one, according to the meaning of his name in Chinese, had no toes and was grotesque. However, all three were great minds. Their fame spread far and wide. Wang Tai caused Confucius to prostrate himself before him. Shen Tujia drove the Prime Minister of the Kingdom of Zheng feel ashamed to show his face. Ai Taita made Duke Ai of Lu willingly offer his throne to him. The brains of these three great minds were not good servants to the organs of the body. They did not take diligent care of all the parts of the body, yet they realised the value of life to its full potential. These talented people were extreme examples. Readers are not prepared to imitate them.

Turning to Look Back

Writing articles on the theme of history entails turning to look back.

In order to be able to turn and look back, one first requires a conception of history. By "conception of history" we mean examining themes and figures in bygone dynasties according to our viewpoint and position.

Almost all of the bygone dynasties were overthrown by another. This embodies the basic relationship between regimes in Chinese history. The replacing of one dynasty by the next, if put in a lighthearted way, can be called "turning over a new leaf". Even so, the finger that turned over that leaf was far from lighthearted in spirit. All considerations of keeping face had to be laid aside, together with feuds, murders and slayings. Power had to sprout from the barrel of a gun, and ordinary people suffered through endless gales of blood.

Our history is a dynastic one, sliced into twenty-five natural portions. There is a simile that likens the annals of China to a long river. One clause should be added to this. Along the course of this long river there are twenty-four dams. These portions were sliced up by the scalpel of politics. Traditions, politics, and still provide continuity between these fragments. Politics and culture share the work and help each other at these crucial crossroads.

From a modern viewpoint, the monarchs who paid sufficient attention to the legacy and the transitions between former dynasties are the so-called "diligent emperors". The

Yuan Dynasty (1279–1368 AD) did not perform well in this respect. Its leaders failed to adequately scrutinise the circumstances behind its overthrow of the Song Dynasty (960–1279 AD). More significantly, they neglected the tradition of blood lineage. In the early years of the Yuan Dynasty, more than half of the local officials did not even understand Mandarin. When meetings were held, interpreters were required, much as they are in an international conference today. The work of uniting and encouraging the hearts of the people mainly relied on various song and dance spectacles, as well as operatic events. Nonetheless, this also stimulated their contribution to the history of Chinese literature. *The Melodies of the Yuan Dynasty* became the apogee of culture to date.

When song, dance and opera compose the main channel for culture in a dynasty it could be said that this dynasty is romantic, but, casting a more critical eye, we can observe that the administrators of Yuan were not familiar with Chinese history. The Qing Dynasty (1644–1912) was similarly controlled by ethnic minorities. It was jointly administered by Manchus and Mongolians. They drew lessons from the previous regimes, paid great attention to the inheritance and fusion of culture, and conducted many specific projects. One of them was to sort out and compile three great books. They were the *Kangxi Dictionary*, the *Collections of Books Past and Present*, and the *Complete Library in the Four Branches of Literature*. To use the words of the present administration, these three great books were the "key cultural projects".

In order to walk forward in a more productive way, one needs to turn and look back. It is vital to keep a clear mind. Where there is no positive sense of purpose, one searches instead for a negative sense of purpose and thus slides from the mire of the present into the whirlpool of history.

Position means the angle through which a person looks at a problem. One true example of this springs to mind. When we were chatting, Mr Jia Pingwa, the Editor-in-Chief of our magazine, told me that in a tiny out-of-the-way village deep in the mountains of Guizhou Province the talented son of a poor family was granted admission to a key university. After he completed his PhD he was assigned to work in Beijing. The young man was extremely duteous to his family. He invited his parents to live in Beijing, but time and again he had difficulty persuading them. The villagers asked the father: "Beijing is not good, is it?" He answered: "Beijing is really good. It is just that it is too far away. It would take days to get there."

The writing of historical prose is biased in that one follows either the way of the blind man who gropes at the elephant or else the frog who sits narrow-mindedly at the bottom of the well. A Tang Dynasty poem states how: "The white-haired lady-in-waiting is still alive/ She talks idly about the Emperor Xuanzong." This kind of record is too sentimental. Talking about history in a playful or random way is only acceptable for entertainment. It is not proper to regard it as a serious literary mode.

Eradicating Desire

Desire is a positive force. It endows life with significance.

Desire is natural. When you are hungry you eat, when you are thirsty you drink, and when the weather is cold you put on extra clothes. Overcome with tiredness you allow yourself a rest, and when exhausted you seek out a pillow. If your body is in its prime you naturally begin to hanker after your wife. From commoners to nobility, from the humble to the exalted, desire is the driver. But desire also has its boundaries. When cooking a meal, if the fire rages too fiercely the food will be scorched or the kitchen might even be engulfed in a blaze. This is surpassing the safe boundaries.

Chinese emperors had their magnificence, but they had their venal side as well. Take for example the profession of a eunuch. In ancient times, men engaged in the central government civil service were compelled to be castrated. In Shaanxi dialect we call this "tearing off power" (*qu shi*). This expression is graphic and direct. Remove the fundamental aspects of a man and you reduce him to a husk devoid of vitality. His figure and force could not be described as winsome. A eunuch is the maleficent seed of the emperor's overblown desire.

If the emperor, like ordinary men, only married one wife, eunuchs could surely be allowed to retain both their figure and their force. The poet Su Shi (1037–1101) famously said: "The toughest task in life is to curb one's desire." The branches of a tree must be pollarded if it is to develop a sturdier trunk. When a normal person gains eminence, he should be swift to restrain himself. Emperors ought to take the lead in managing their desire. Common folk only singe their own fingers with desire, yet the monarch's desire can set the whole country alight.

Curbing desire may be tough, but what kind of desire should be curbed? To what extent should it be curbed? This is troublesome to determine. The character of the Pig in *The Journey to the West* curbed none of his desires. Hence, he became a laughing stock. A monk shaves his head, uprooting what was on his head and in his mind. He turns his back on worldly life. That is onerous. Only men of a particular disposition can achieve it. It would be more difficult still for an emperor to curb his desire. He might say: "I ate shit and drank piss to get where I am. Was that a walk in the park for me?"

One episode of the TV serial *The Emperor Kangxi* features a song which states: "I really want to live for another five centuries." He was the emperor, so he was bound to harbour this aspiration. As for the suffering masses, they would not want to endure tomorrow. The Emperor Kangxi (reigned 1661–1722 AD) was a mound of jollity. The dramatisation of his life ascribed to him a host of talents and virtues. In today's society with its fledgling democracy, it is ill-advised to rhapsodise about the greatness of a past monarch.

A human lifespan may not exceed one hundred years. Those with a hasty temperament might be short-lived, whereas those with an iron stomach could well prolong their existence. The heavens weigh up every factor when ordaining the number of our days on Earth. A man of sixty or seventy has weathered almost every conceivable circumstance. Once he has seen them all through, he is obliged to retire. His "life experience" must be bequeathed to the next generation. At this critical moment, the heavens engineer a new phenomenon in the chain of being, known as the "generation gap". The younger folk refute the lessons of their elders. They are apt to explore every situation for themselves, suffering and enduring the selfsame tribulations as their predecessors. The somersaults of life have to be rehearsed from scratch. The generation gap concurs with the Scientific Outlook on Development as it serves to prevent the rate of human evolution accelerating too fast.

Let us imagine that humans had a life expectancy of three hundred years with two hundred and sixty set as the retirement age. Most of the people walking out on the streets or sitting at home would be ghostly shells. The human race could not have persisted until now. It would have long been consigned to extinction. From this perspective, we can see that the heavens too are at pains to curb their desire. In limiting our mortal lives to a more modest span, they have enacted their own stroke of genius.

"At any point there is multiplication and division in life." So runs a line from a poem by Zeng Guofan (1811–72). Zeng was not a master poet and most of his verses are philosophical in character. His poems of ideas cannot hold a candle to those of Su Shi. Nonetheless, Su Shi had no knowledge of combat or of leading military forces, nor could he take control of his own life. His poems improved exponentially as he went along, in diametric opposition to his lot as an official. He was repeatedly exiled and so belonged to that group of people who defy the logic of metaphysics. In the sphere of human desires, he demonstrated a shred of self-control. By contrast, Wang Wei (699–759 AD) and Bai Juyi (772–846 AD) struck a balance between creative effulgence and an aptitude for office. Consequently, they were blessed with long lives and could savour the whole gustatory gamut from fish to bears paws.

Men die seeking their fortune and birds are killed for the plate. Family life encompasses the patient accumulation of property. From being adequately clothed and fed to being fairly well-off is a basic process of addition. Those who strike gold overnight are working miracles of multiplication. In an orderly and systematic society, addition is the main arithmetical stratagem. In an era of disorder and chaos, multiplication takes over. This is suggested by the saying "a chaotic world breeds heroes". A chaotic world not only refers to one riven by war and skirmishes, where the populace has no sanctuary. If a prosperous society lacks order and system, it cannot claim that its politics are transparent and well-defined.

When we are undertaking division, we take subtraction as our starting point. Subtractions are also gruelling. As for money, the more the better. As for fame, the greater the better. As for one's official position, the higher the better. A man "rises with the cock's crow" and returns "shouldering a hoe under the moonlight". Those three expressions – money, fame and official position – keep him occupied from dawn to nightfall. That is until one day he succumbs to fatigue and cannot get out of bed. It would be futile then for him to curse that trio in his heart. But, on making a mild recovery, he again sets out in pursuit of them.

An old chestnut relates how an elderly landlord nearing death could not close his eyes for several days, but still managed to raise two fingers. His children and grandchildren could not make out what he was trying to communicate. His wife, having been his lifelong companion, blew out one of their two oil lamps. The landlord then lowered his hand and passed away. This kind of person is both loathsome and endearing. He truly carried his life's preoccupation right up until the very end.

Thieves in the Heart

"It is easy to capture thieves in the mountains, but not the thieves in your heart." So opined the great philosopher Wang Yangming (1472–1529 AD).

His words have a ring of truthfulness. Even though the human heart is made of flesh, this piece of flesh is expansive, refined and inscrutable. It is loftier than the sky, thicker than the earth, deeper than the oceans, hotter than fire, more precious than gold, chillier than ice, tougher than iron, and thinner than a leaf of paper. Every single change in the world has its origins and resolution in this piece of flesh. An ancient couplet describes it thus: –

Among the hundreds of varieties of goodness, filial piety ranks the best; it is revealed through the heart rather than works; otherwise poor families would be utterly bereft /

Among the hundreds of varieties of evil, obscenity ranks the worst; it is revealed through works rather than the heart; otherwise there would be few perfect men left.

Thieves in the heart were the original sin. In Buddhism this is known as "evil intentions" (*e'nian*). These include murder, robbery and obscenity and are all concerned with the body. Lies, profane words, having a forked tongue, and swearing are all concerned with the mouth. Greed, anger, and addiction are all concerned with the mind. More than a decade ago, Jia Pingwa wrote out eight characters on his bookshelves:

"Bridle your mouth socially; Bridle thoughts in solitude." In recent days, Xi'an has seen constant downpours. Houses have been leaking. When I went to inspect his office in the morning, those eight characters remained fresh and striking.

The Qing Dynasty minister Ji Xiaolan (1724–1805) delineated two types of thieves in the heart. One features in the tale of a rich lady by the name of Madame Zhang. She kept a spotted lapdog. As she was long in the tooth, she asked her housemaids to look after it. Life wore on peacefully. The story proper begins with the repeated disappearance of meat from the kitchen. The maids suspected that the dog was the culprit, so made a secret pact to kill it. Days after the deed was done, it still cast a shadow over them. One of the girls, the comely Willow Yi, was afflicted by recurring nightmares. In her dream murdered dog was chasing after her and sinking its teeth into her flesh. When Madame Zhang learned about this, she shared a pearl of wisdom: "You maids conspired together to slay a pet, but why is only Willow Yi plagued with guilt? Obviously, she was the actual meat thief. The animal realised the injustice of it all." Willow Yi was hauled over for cross-examination. It turned out that the allegation was correct. Evil cannot be hidden. According to traditional concepts, evil is to be disliked, but hidden evil is to be totally abhorred.

The second story relates what happened to an aged scholar. In ancient times, such a personage bore the title of "learned Confucian". One night, the God of Death sent his henchmen over to capture this particular man of letters. Believing that his days had come to an end, he followed them. On reaching hell and examining the Book of Life and Death, they discovered that they had accosted the wrong person. Fearlessly, the aged scholar asked for this aberration to be rectified. The City God, who was the local presiding judge, expressed his apologies and commanded that the henchmen be lashed with twenty rods. The aged scholar had long enjoyed a reputation for withholding forgiveness even from those who admitted their guilt. Even in the depths of hell, he would not show mercy to these spirits.

Duly, the chief justice, the God of Death, came along to settle the matter. He said: "The muddleheaded henchmen are to blame for your manhandling. Their absentmindedness caused this. No serious harm has been done. This is not like in the world of mortals where officials frame people on purpose. Distinguished old sir, please raise your noble hand and forgive them. 'Even the planets do not orbit in perfect circles, much less are ghosts and spirits infallible'." In the eyes of the God of Death, the deciding factor was whether there was any ulterior motive or not.

Not so long ago, I heard a new story. A wealthy surgeon established a company and invited his middle school classmate to serve as the director of the board. The position was a sinecure and he could claim 50,000 RMB per annum without ever having to set foot inside the office. That man had been laid off and was on his uppers, beset with every kind of worry. This offer came as timely rain. He thought that the iron tree was about to break into blossom and his luck would alter on reaching middle age. With profound gratitude he accepted the certificate of appointment. Henceforth, wherever he went, he would gush panegyrics of praise about his old classmate, claiming that he was the only competent surgeon in the whole city and the rest were just butchers.

A few years passed by and accusations of business malpractice were levelled at the company. As director of the board, the said man was fingered as the prime suspect. The timely rain had become June snow. He wanted to weep, but there were no tears in his eyes. After all, for ages he had been receiving a stipend from the business. His classmate was still his classmate and the surgeon was still a surgeon. Only now, he faced incarceration.

I repeated this story to Mr Jia Pingwa and, at the same time, raised the topic of thieves in the heart. He replied that he had once been to a village where he saw a derelict temple dedicated to the God of the Earth. The couplet on its front gate had almost been worn away, but the letters were still legible in outline. It read:

This one street is rife with quips;

We two seniors should brace our lips.

Knowing How to Talk

The mouth is a tool. Its main functions are eating, drinking and talking. As for its other uses, that is down to personal yen. One may, for instance, play the flute, blow the panpipes, blast away on the *suona* horn, ply a kiss, or puff on a kiss, and so on.

It is better to speak frankly. Those who prevaricate never make themselves popular. Even so, on some choice occasions, the art of speech warrants attention. Learning to talk really is a must.

I should like to recount three anecdotes concerning exchanges between kings and their ministers.

Yan Ying was a high official in the State of Qi. His position was on a par with that of a prime minister. One subject of the state caused offence to King Jinggong (died 490 BC) and found himself bound up in ropes and hauled before the Great Hall of the Court. Jinggong wielded his celestial prestige, decreeing that this blackguard be torn limb from limb. The King, moreover, bellowed that whoever dared speak in the condemned man's defense would likewise forfeit their life. Yan Ying rolled up his sleeves and drew his dagger. He placed his left hand on the prisoner's head and sharpened the blade – *hou, hou, hou* – with his right hand. He asked the King in a raised voice: "Your Majesty, when the just and sainted kings of old wanted to dismember convicts, where did they dig the knife in first?" On hearing these words, Jinggong answered: "Let him go. The fault is mine."

Jian Yong was the "Foreign Minister" under the Emperor

Xuande of Shu-Han (Liu Bei, 223–221 BC). He was a distinctly learned man, especially in the eyes of his master. Whenever any business was discussed in the Royal Court, he would be seated in a designated position just to the side of the famed general Zhuge Liang. One year, a serious drought struck the State of Shu. The government issued a decree prohibiting the private distillation of liquor. Perhaps this was a water conservation measure. In the process of enforcing the law, the officials apprehended a number of people secretly harbouring stills and other contraband equipment at home. They prepared to mete out the punishments stipulated for this crime. One day Jian Yong and the Emperor Xuande happened to be walking the streets, making an inspection in nondescript plain clothes. They caught sight of a man and a woman laughing and conversing together at leisure. Jian Yong said: "This pair is going to commit an obscene act and should be arrested at once." Xuande probed: "How do you know?" Jian Yong replied: "They have the tools fit for the purpose." The Emperor burst into laughter and ordered that all those found with spirit-making paraphernalia be let free.

Sometimes silence is more potent than words. The wet nurse to the Emperor Wu of Han (Liu Che, reigned 141–87 BC) was complacent about currying the favour of her superiors. As such, she broke the law indiscriminately. The news of her actions ignited Wu's fury and he wanted to punish her to death. In a bid to save her life, the wet nurse went to Dong Fangsu for help. The "straw of hope" Dong extended to her was that: "No matter how seriously the Emperor scolds you, just listen and do not be contrary. When the Emperor orders that you be sent down, you should hold your tongue. Just turn your head back and try to fix him in the face. So much the better if tears are welling up in your eyes." The wet nurse did as she was instructed. The human heart is a thing of flesh. The gratitude felt for the one who suckled you must be higher than the skies and deeper than the oceans. That piece of tender flesh inside Wu's breast was touched. "The sadness was too much for the Emperor to bear. He granted her a reprieve."

The history of Chinese politics has two guiding threads. One is the thread belonging to emperors. The other is that belonging to prime ministers. The imperial thread is an arc because he is part of a household contract system. The personal aptitude of monarchs varies immensely. The prime ministerial thread is linear. They all swim in the highest stream. Good emperors are served by capable ministers, whereas incompetent emperors find themselves falling at their mercy. The ruler's words are authoritative, so they set no store by the art of talking. Prime ministers, however, rely on two qualities – knowing how to run a tight ship and knowing how to talk. In history, countless ministers and eminent imperial physicians lost their heads because they were in want of tact.

The mouth is a tool. It can be employed as a megaphone. In eating, it is a bucket for food. Its true covert bosses are the heart and brain. "Speak with a clear conscience" and "loose talk is witless talk" – these two everyday sayings bear this out. Writing an article is in fact a form of speech; only an alternative set of tools are wielded. The pen is substituted for the mouth. I believe that the following five criteria are all one needs to compose a top-notch article: speak human words, speak true words, speak household words, speak sincere words, and speak words with personality and wisdom.

Price and Cost

There is a price and a cost behind a country's progress.

The best way to resist change is to relinquish communication and seal off a society from the outside world. The Chinese behaved like this prior to the fall of the Qing Dynasty (1644–1912). All of the foreign envoys were considered to have come to China to demonstrate their fealty. Communication involves mutual respect, though the core value of communication is to construct a system of self-renewal and to cultivate one's strength. The Great Qing Dynasty perished because of its isolationism. The exchanges that occurred subsequently caused the Chinese people to lose face. The twentieth century was the only one in the history of the Great Cathay in which she was forced to surrender her confident front. Whether they came from the East or the West, all those goods originating from abroad – foreign vehicles, foreign matches, foreign candles and foreign paraffin – plugged almost every crevice in Chinese society. Even to this day, there is a predilection for foreign articles, be it in the names of newly-built projects by commercial construction companies or the theories taught in university classes.

The pitfall in bilateral exchanges lies in the possibility that all national genetic information may be lost. It is a little like employing GM technology to alter the seed of a plant. Indeed "making foreign things serve China" did deliver great changes to us, including economic prosperity and political justice. On account of this profound development, there is an ever-pressing need to fortify traditional

Chinese elements. The universities within a country, especially in the field of the humanities, feel that if one's own traditional elements cannot be made to hold sway, then the outcome will be lamentable for future generations.

On 26th September 1792, three large ships carrying 700 British envoys embarked from Portsmouth. Their destination was China. The leader of the delegation was Lord Macartney. On 14th September 1793, the Emperor Qianlong greeted the visitors in "a curtained chamber illuminated by paper lanterns". The twelve-year-old boy who lifted the cloak and the lower hem of Macartney's outfit was named Thomas Staunton and it was he who was to trigger war between the two nations as an adult. A prodigy, he purportedly picked up the Chinese language from the missionary interpreter on the voyage over. Qianlong's dragon face lit up upon hearing his "fluent Chinese". He "unfastened the yellow silken pouch from his waistband and in an unprecedented gesture bestowed it upon the boy". Together with the huge delegation, the newly-invented steam engine, the mechanised spinning frame and loom, and the hot air balloon, were introduced to China. The Emperor Qianlong's reaction was that his Celestial Court was in want of nothing. In return, he presented a carved jade mace intended for the King of England and a jade wand for Macartney.

Twenty-four years later, on the 28th August 1816, the second British envoy arrived in Peking. The head of the delegation was Lord Amherst, with the now thirty-six-year-old Thomas Staunton as his deputy. Staunton had been residing in Canton for many years as a representative of the British East India Company. However, the Emperor Jiaqing refused to meet them and had the party driven away. The official record states: "Cathay is the master of all under heaven. It cannot tolerate such proud and supercilious behaviour. I ordered that should they retreat with haste; they will not be punished for their heinous incursion." Popular retellings of the story proffer two explanations for this. One is that that British envoy declined to kneel down three times and kowtow nine times upon being received by the Emperor. The other is that Staunton was known to be a merchant. An emperor could not condescend to entertain an individual of his stripe.

Another twenty odd years passed by. On 7th April 1840, the almost sixty-year-old Thomas Staunton declared in the British House of Commons with vehemence and excitement that: "The question between us and the Chinese government with regard to the opium trade was not a question of morality or policy, but a question whether there had been any breach of international rights or international law [...] Undoubtedly, the Chinese government had a right to carry their laws into more stringent effect, and it was for foreigners then to inquire what those laws were and obey them. [...] When the imperial commissioner arrived at Canton he brought with him a new law of a very extraordinary and severe character, a law denouncing death against any foreigner who traded in opium, and subjecting his property to confiscation to the crown. [...] There was no law before in China by which the hair of the head of any European could have been touched for smuggling. Let the House recollect that our empire in the East was founded on the force of opinion; if we submitted to the degrading insults of China, the time would not be far distant when our political ascendancy in India would be at an end." Hansard further recorded how Staunton "very reluctantly" lent his assent to armed resistance, affirming: "This war was absolutely just and necessary, under existing circumstances, [and] he rejoiced to find that it had received the tacit approbation of that House." One hundred and seventy years ago, this is what the British people believed a just war to be.

In June 1840, a fleet made up of forty ships carrying four hundred soldiers docked at Canton, having passed through Bangladesh. From then on, the Chinese people were compelled to begin their lives without any face to lose.

Crying Uncle

To "cry uncle" (*jiao yeye*) is a dialect expression, a local phrase.

One man may insult another, strike him with his fist and ask: "Ready to give in or not?" The victim is then spread-eagled with his head against the ground and a mouthful of mud, struggling to raise his neck in resistance. With another punch comes the threat: "Come on. Do you surrender or not?" Still twisting his neck, he is dealt another three or five punches. Finally, his head wilts to the earth in resignation. To cry uncle is to surrender, to admit defeat. An alternative outcome is conceivable, though. The victim might opt to take a step back, to remove himself from the altercation, his rationale being that: "Paths wind through mountains and when the willow is dark the flowers are bright."

There is another saying, "as silly as an ox". Why is an ox silly? The beast is stubborn, steadfast, hardworking and resilient, and mostly consigns itself to silence. All of these attributes do not amount to silliness. If you strum a lute for the ox's amusement, it is not the animal but the person who is daft. The ox is only silly because it allows itself to be led along by the snout. Once a rope has been looped through its nostrils, the behemoth can be steered, even by a child. The youngster may, furthermore, mount its back and fool around on a flute. Regrettably were there not somebody to take the lead, the ox would be clueless as to which direction it should go. Old nags remember their bearings, but oxen are bewildered.

Saddam Hussein and Colonel Gaddafi were resolute and

forcible leaders. Right up until he was lynched, Saddam never gave his ground, kept a calm countenance and raised his head up high. Gaddafi too refused to give an inch. And yet there was one tangible difference between these contemporaries. Saddam had no illusions about the West. In 1969, Gaddafi overthrew the regime of King Idris, who was supported by Britain and the US. He established the Republic of Libya, demolished the US Villiers military base and drove away British Petroleum. In fact, he continued to shield American oil interests, even placing the company headquarters under government protection.

In December 2003, Libya declared that they had abandoned their "weapons of mass destruction development programme". In January 2004, the country's nuclear devices and research equipment were transferred to an "exhibition" in the US. On 23rd March, the US Assistant Secretary of State William Burns visited Libya. When he met with Gaddafi, he "handed him a letter from President Bush". On 25th March, Tony Blair arrived in Libya. In 2006, America declared the full restoration of diplomatic relations with the nation. Moreover, they expunged Libya's name from the list of "countries known to support terrorism". In December 2007, at the invitation of the newly-elected President Sarkozy, Gaddafi was granted a five-day trip to France, during which he signed a raft of concords and contracts with "a total value of 10 billion Euros". These included the purchase of twenty-one airbuses. At that time, Sarkozy stated publicly: "Among the leaders of the Arab nations France does not regard Gaddafi as a dictator. He is the longest-serving president in the region. In the Arab world this is a matter of huge significance." In 2009, Gaddafi arrived in New York City and attended the United Nations

Congress. On 19th March 2011, France, America and Britain launched a seaborne air attack on Libya. Within three days, hundreds of missiles "visited" the land of Libya. When Gaddafi first learned that the French fighter jets had been at the vanguard, he said off the cuff: "Sarkozy is my friend. I think he must have gone crazy."

I have a British friend who teaches at a university in Xi'an. He is fond of the Shaanxi History Museum. He has been around the exhibition halls scores of times. Every time he meets me, he enthuses with relish about the curios he has come across. Once when we were chatting, I said: "There's one vital detail that you have overlooked." He listened, all ears. "Museums represent the condensed history of the civilisation of a country. Each relic has its own origin and tale to share. They are the cumulative memory of the nation. Every last piece in that museum is ours, with not one iota from abroad. The British Museum cannot make the same boast." He nodded in embarrassment and conceded this was true.

In another conversation, I cracked a joke: "The G8 is an eight-nation alliance, referred to humorously as 'the wealthy nations club'. Its members include America, Britain, France, Germany, Italy, Canada, Japan and Russia. If we replace Canada with the Austro-Hungarian Empire, they are the same countries who formed the Eight-Power Allied Force that sacked Peking and torched the Summer Palace."

The history of a country's civilisation is a compound structure. It is somewhat like a set of scales. Justice is at one end and might at the other. If one end or the other falters, the nation is plunged into a state of imbalance.

Two Reflections on the Great Helmsman

I. THE REVELATION OF THE LEADER'S BUST

A novelist friend of mine has two statues on display in his study. One is of Guanyin, the other is of Mao Zedong.

The effigy of Guanyin measures only eight inches tall. It has been in the world of man for several hundred years. The greater portion of its surface has lost its sheen and become worn. Some areas, such as the top of the head, the chin and shoulders have had furrows chafed into them through the constant rubbing of mortal hands. Perhaps these developed as the statue was frequently moved here and there. Guanyin is depicted stepping on a lotus flower, her supercilious gaze penetrating beyond this world. Hers is an unearthly talent. By comparison, the likeness of Mao Zedong seems to be a denizen of the sublunary world. His eyes glisten brightly as though surveying omnisciently from a commanding height. The statue of Mao is a bust, a foot tall, broad-shouldered and broad-chested. His uniform, styled after that of Sun Yat-sen, reflects the bearing of a leader. This kind of bust is seldom seen now, but was in vogue during the Cultural Revolution and virtually every family had one. They would display it in the most prominent position in the living room to demonstrate the loyalty of the household to the great leader.

The statue of Guanyin is cast in bronze, whereas that of Mao is molded from fine porcelain. My friend told me:

"The Guanyin is a family heirloom. It has gathered the dust of my forefathers for five generations. The model of Mao was something I pilfered myself. I intend to hand both of them on to the younger generation."

He recounted the story of the bust.

In the spring of 1986, he went to his hometown of Qiqihaer to visit his parents. When chatting with his father in the evening, the old man excitedly let it slip that a "secret decision" had been made in his work unit that afternoon. His father was the Party Secretary of the Supply and Sales Department. They had in their possession two barns, the largest of which had been sealed for a dozen years. It was chockfull of busts of Mao Zedong put into storage by the biggest troop of Red Guards. Nobody knew why they had been left there – nobody thought to ask.

After the Reform and Opening-up to the outside world, the circulation of commercial goods improved miraculously so storage space was now at a premium. Their work unit held "discussions" about how the largest barn should be put to use. Nearly six years elapsed and a solution had not been reached. When they sought the opinion of their superiors, they merely received a verbal response telling them to sort it out by themselves.

They wanted to build another storeroom from scratch, but there wasn't enough vacant land. Furthermore, the statues of the great leader could not be relocated to the courtyard, since this would leave them exposed to weathering from gales and downpours. Following many rounds of consideration, the "heads of the unit" gritted their teeth and released a privately-reached decision: in order to free up storage room and improve economic prosperity the stored "artefacts" would be broken up. The working staff at the unit were unwilling to perform this task. The heads of the unit did not wish to shoulder the responsibility either. Hence, they offered up a 200 yuan payment to a pack of "hoodlums" off the street to do the smashing. The operation was to be carried out under top secrecy the following evening.

The next day after dinner, my friend went to the barn. The "hoodlums" were already there. He didn't heed the instructions and, before the men sprang into action, he handed over ten yuan in exchange for one of the ceramic heads.

This bust "snatched from the jaws of death" was placed alongside the bronze Guanyin on top of one of the bookshelves in his study.

II. THE FAITH OF CAB DRIVERS

Faith is something that seems more lucid the further you are removed from it. One cannot draw too close to it, otherwise it putrefies into desire. Most of the totems revered in folk customs are in fact objects of desire. We fixate on the idea of "whatever we pray for will be granted" and "making vows before god" and "having those vows redeemed". Fishermen worship the God of the Sea and the God of the Rivers, mountaineers worship the Mountain God, farmers worship the God of the Earth, those who are childless worship the Guanyin of Fertility, and those who are short of money worship the God of Fortune. Thus, we normally pay no attention to theological deities because those gods offer moral guidance for human subjects and not "practical favours". To put this bluntly, we are a nation of pragmatists. We do not revere the Yellow Emperor even though we claim to be his progeny. Most Chinese (apart from natives of Shaanxi) do not even know who the Yellow Emperor was.

I first encountered the "Mao Boom" when travelling in a cab. This was in Xi'an in the early part of November 1990. At the time, I was studying in the Writers' Workshop at Northwest University. That day I arrived in the city by train and by the time I alighted it was already midnight. The public bus service had long since ceased. I hailed a taxi. Were it not so cold and so late, and were I not in such an exhausted state, I would not have gone to this expense.

Soon after the cab set off, I found myself transfixed by the portrait of the Great Helmsman propped against the windscreen. It was a likeness in brittle plastic, different from the run of the mill cards we grew used to seeing later on. Its surfaces were decorated with fluorescent powder. Whenever light struck it from the back or the side, Chairman Mao would bedazzle. According to the cab driver, it was given to him as a gift by a Hong Kong businessman. I don't know whether that was true or not. Such pictures in due course became a common sight, cropping up in taxis, on shop shelves and even being peddled out on the streets. Later still, almost all of the vehicles, including cabs and official cars, had these delicate and eye-catching pictures on display. The one I observed in Xi'an was certainly the most beguiling.

My chat with the cab driver left a deep impression on me. I asked him, half-jokingly: "You've stuck Chairman Mao's portrait in front of you – do you want him to bless you with a fortune or lead you in the right direction?"

The driver was about forty years old with a strong Xi'an accent. "I started to drive when Chairman Mao was still alive. At that time, my family was not rich, though they could claim to be slightly better off than others. My father drove as well. I wouldn't expect Chairman Mao to reward me with a fortune." He turned around and grinned at me, then carried on jovially: "Chairman Mao did not scrape along well with the rich. He was the same his whole life long. He was the great saviour in the eyes of the poor. I have been driving off my own bat for seven or eight years. You can survey all the people in Xi'an. I must have been one of the pioneers – one of the first to work as a freelancer. As far as money is concerned, I am not loaded, but have a bit stashed away. As far as life is concerned, everyone needs faith. Am I correct?"

Before I was able to answer him, he continued: "Chairman Mao made people believe in him – a pillar of justice and fairness." He tapped the plastic card with his fingertip. "I place it here because watching it makes me feel calm and centred."

You can see that the cabby's reverence for Chairman Mao was something chosen after a careful process of selection. It arose from the bottom of his heart. People's passions are natural and cannot be stirred under duress. From this I inferred that whenever a person or an idea becomes popular propaganda but does not have to face one scrap of resistance, then its influence is superficial. It is not bred in the heart.

To Write Prose is to Speak Human Words

Prose is a form of speech. One can only speak in human language, using words which are truthful and meant sincerely.

To speak in human language means to not speak in the language of the gods unless you are a heavenly being. Do not utter the language of ghosts unless you are the Grim Reaper. What is more, do not adopt the tone of an official. Even if you are in fact an official, you should not put on airs. The air of an official can be vented in the realms of officialdom, but when it comes to prose writing, such haughtiness ought to be kept under wraps. Avoid the language of dreams as well. Writing is the distillation of thousands of years of praxis. Compose articles when you are sober-minded; express yourself in the manner of a normal and hale person.

Empty words are not truthful. Truthful words are solid, fecund and close to reality. Solidity implies the opposite of emptiness and connotes the use of authentic content. Fecund denotes having a positive outcome. Fine articles convey fine reasoning and fine thought. When a farmer tends his crops, he is mindful of both the daily growth and the ultimate harvest. Literary writing should focus on reality too and, in fact, cling to it. Clinging to reality does not infer clapping one's palms and declaiming a message loudly. It should not only register the pulse of the age, but moreover grasp the characteristics, rhythm and trends therein. What then are social trends? The folk proverb, "Thirty years on the east bank of the river, and thirty years on the west", rings quite true. Let us take the last century as a point of reference. From 1919 to 1949, thirty years elapsed, and from 1949 to 1979 another thirty years went by. During these two phases of three decades, the changes were so acute that the heavens and the earth seemed to have shifted places.

True words are also solid words, which prove effective and practical. True words wear no showy garb, nor do they dress up or have the appearance of an actor. True words may sound unpleasant. They might even grate on one's ears. True words can raise the hackles of "big shots". They are rare because they are innovative and share a fresh understanding of the world.

Solid words can be stated in a solid manner. They can, moreover, make use of analogy and example. When ill-tempered and conceited listeners are present, solid words may provide a means of sugaring a bitter pill. Nonetheless, no matter how one uses them, the speaker should maintain a calm mind. Speaking in high spirits, with one's fists waving and ankles springing, or gasping for breath, or one's hair on end and flushed with anger – these are the battery of rich emotions an orator can deploy. If one simply speaks for the sake of self-satisfaction and to unload personal discontent, it becomes like a song and dance routine. On balance, it is not healthy to cultivate such a habit. The body is over-taxed by this.

True words are not vaunted but ordinary. If in a particular era, telling the truth is regarded as a rare practice or as a sign of noble character, then that period and society must be benighted. By scanning the newspapers, watching television broadcasts, listening to the radio and skimming through magazines, it is very easy to gauge whether a society is benighted and sad or not. In order to build a civilised society, a basic and sincere etiquette must be cultivated in much the same way as these qualities are nurtured in writing. Having a civilised society does not mean that every day is like a festival and that swallows and warblers cavort and twitter all over the place. Rather, the people are caressed by a smooth and gentle breeze and can cleave to a sense of safety and inner calm.

Speaking sincere words implies you have principles and boundaries. In life, people dislike those who talk big. Big talk is not empty talk, but endless ranting without limits. The power of the Buddha is boundless. He can declaim big words, whereas human beings cannot. Articles are written for people to read; words are spoken for people to hear. Thus, the content must be sincere and acceptable. Sincere words are household words. "The aged monk only speaks in household words", while novices always have the *sutras* in their hands and on their lips. "Never show your whole heart; only share thirty per cent of what is in your mind." This refers to words spoken to strangers on the street. They are exchanged out of politeness and are not household words *per se*.

In writing a piece of prose, one must cherish the vocabulary. A marksman cherishes the weapon in his hands. The ancient Chinese language was broad and profound, elegant and substantial. Modern Chinese only stretches back a hundred years. For a man, living a century represents great longevity. For a language shared by over one billion people, it is still juvenile. Because of this juvenility, it requires more solicitude.

Tracing back the developmental journey of Modern Chinese, we need to be critical on two basic points. One concerns an inferiority complex. When the use of vernacular Chinese was advocated, the country was in what ought to be considered a state of acute backwardness and confusion when set against the great sweep of its history. We tried to learn more from abroad, but in fact absorbed less from our own ancient heritage. Even now, this casts a shadow over our psychology. Some improper and half-digested loanwords remain popular. These days, when we emphasise the building of cultural confidence, there are too many basic elements which need to be re-examined.

The other factor is that literary style bears the impress of "ne'er do well" politics. What is "ne'er do well" politics? Let me cite several sentences from China's 1970 "New Year's Pledge". One glance is enough. "The 1960s have been and gone. All the proletariat and revolutionary masses of the world have strode proudly and belligerently into the great 1970s. Surveying the entire world with an eye to the future, peoples of every ethnic group in our nation are propelled by waves of emotion […]. In the past decade, our enemies have grown more cankerous by the day. We have grown better by the day […]. During these ten years, under the new conditions the proletariat and the mass revolutionary movement have spread throughout the globe with the power of almighty thunder and the zeal to topple mountains and overturn the seas. The waves of the national liberation movement are surging on higher and higher." This style of language is superficial with too much surface ornament and too little core. It is emotional, even irrational. In this barrage of verbiage, the vocabulary is not cherished in the least. The modern Chinese language is the basic material for modern Chinese literature. In constructing a grand building, the basic materials should not be merely adequate, but of premium quality.

The literary criteria for prose writing in the present day are not so clear. Beyond the overall concept of prose, there is the essay, the literary note and the sketch. As for fiction, there is the novel, the novella and the short story. For poetry, there are lyric, philosophical and narrative divisions. As far as the connotations of prose are concerned, its definitions are confusing. We are waiting for a theoretical combing and cognition to be initiated in this research field. Another fact must be taken into account. Namely, if we sweep away all Western theories from the study of literature, very little is left behind. The status quo of contemporary literary studies is somewhat like the automobile industry. The complete assembly line was imported. We did not achieve the target of being "made in China". That is to say, we have yet to establish a contemporary system for literary evaluation based on Chinese modes of thinking.

Not only in the field of literary studies, but in numerous others do we lack our own self-defined benchmarks. China's aggregate economy ranks second in the world. This sprawling achievement has been made since we opened up to the outside world. Still, the criteria for this ranking were determined according to Western standards. For every index and yardstick relating to economics, education, medicine, environmental protection, industry and agriculture, we are bereft of a homespun standard. In building a great nation, we should insist on greatness from the very root. It is high time for us to establish Chinese criteria. This is true of Chinese literature too.

In What Kind of House Did the Jade Emperor Live?

In what kind of house did the Jade Emperor live? In *Journey to the West* the author Wu Cheng'en (c. 1500-82 AD) designed the Jade Emperor's residence according to those inhabited by rulers in the real world. Wu was a *gongsheng* or "senior licentiate" in the reign of the Emperor Jiajing of Ming (1521–67). The highest rank he attained was *xiancheng*, that is to say the assistant to the county head. Now, when writers are sent down to experience life in the provinces they will usually serve in a similar post. Pu Songling (1640–1715), the author of *Strange Tales from the Liaozhai Studio*, worked as a *gongsheng* in the Qing Dynasty. The most senior position he held was as the Director of a Confucian Academy, which is on a par with the deputy head of a Communist Party county school in modern times. The job was a paper one, so his mind was not burdened and he had the leisure to be able to gather anecdotes and amusing stories.

An alternative name for the *gongsheng* was *juren fubang*, or "qualified scholar in waiting". These two superlative authors, whose names are carved into the historical record, did not have first-rate diplomas. What they shared was a comparable manner of thinking and writing. Both of them chose the road less travelled and gave full tilt to their imagination. The ghosts and spirits in their works mimicked the behaviour and lives of ordinary mortal folk. Buddhas may accept a bribe or ghosts might be led astray by passion.

The Jade Emperor is the paramount god. In Wu Cheng'en's

works, his dwelling place is modelled on those of monarchs in this world. This can be construed as something of an affront. Wu's official position was low, so he had no opportunity to witness firsthand the imperial palaces. Thus, he had to rely on his whimsy to sketch a home for the Jade Emperor.

The dialogue between the Emperor and his ministers in the Heavenly Court also imitates its terrestrial counterparts. He was rather familiar with this type of business. He never tasted mutton himself but knew how sheep gamboled. Wu therefore addressed the Jade Emperor as the dear ruler who should "live ten thousand years" (*wansui*). The home of the Emperor was rendered as "the palace" (*gong*), yet in the order of things he could find no proper name for the residence of the immortals whose rank was supposedly higher than this leader of flesh and blood.

Chinese people have a common comprehension of what literature should do. Namely, there is a tendency towards showing imagination while not transgressing boundaries. In the face of their superiors, they are at a loss. In the face of their inferiors, they act as they see fit. For example, in English the residence of the US president is known as the "White House". That carries the connotation of being on an equal footing with the public. Chinese translators favour the expression "White Palace" (*Baigong*). Another example is how in China before an infant is born the womb he inhabits is called the "kid's palace" (*zigong*). This means that in the prenatal stage, everyone is as privileged as an emperor. "The greatest concern of heaven is to foster new life" – this is the Chinese view of life. When a child is born into an ordinary family, his or her birth is described as "tumbling into the grass" (*luocao*) because the majority of people belong to the grassroots (*caomin*).

In ancient times, the novel did not fit into the upper echelons of Chinese society. It was not worthy to be conferred on a grand occasion. The Chinese word for novel is "small talk" (*xiaoshuo*). The prefix "small" is employed not out of modesty or on account of the tiny scale of such a work. "Small talk" enshrines the old view of literature. To set down prose is to "expound one's ideas" (*liyan*) and to "establish an exemplar" (*shuren*). Hence, it was upheld as the apotheosis of literary endeavour. The novel can be counted as a diversion, the contrivance of a leisurely and carefree mood. It belongs absolutely to the preserve of writing for pleasure. To express this in fashionable parlance, prose is about "magnifying one's ego" (*dawo*) whereas the novel is about "masking one's ego" (*xiaowo*). The basic material for every novel composed in China is "tittle-tattle from the streets and alleys". The style is directly influenced by the narrative form of the storytelling script. Consequently, novels are divided into chapters and at the end of each is a statement encouraging the reader to carry on if they want to know what happens next. The ensuing chapter will commence by expressly picking up where the action left off.

More so than any other literature throughout the world, the tales found in ancient Chinese novels entered the repertoire of oral storytellers. The greatest vanity for a writer in the old days was to hear his works issuing from the mouths of such performers. Now, novels strive to arrest the eyes, the greatest aspiration being to spawn a TV or movie adaptation. If an author's work is selected by a director, no matter how renowned he is already the creator will be privately in raptures.

Times have changed. Ancient novels and modern novels are completely different. The novel has now been installed as the apotheosis of literary endeavour. The scribbler of a handful of chapbooks of prose or verse cannot be considered the novelist's peer. The only regrettable matter is how the genre still bears the same name tag. A soldier on the frontline can be called a "scrapping dog" (*ergou*), though on being promoted as a general he must shed such labels.

There are three aspects of the Chinese novel that foreigners find hard to comprehend. The first is the inclusion of supernatural tales. Fairies, foxes or snakes metamorphose into human form. Their purpose is to revel in the beauty of our existence. In fairytales and legends from abroad, it is typically people who are transformed into animals. Some of this magic is the result of sorcery. The resolution of the story marks a victory for justice and the noble conscience, with the changeling restored to his or her former identity as soon as the truth is revealed. In China there is no reversion unless the character commits a mistake or overstretches their power. In either case, the spirits are exasperated and they curtail the adventure as punishment.

It is easy to understand why ghosts should wish to escape their gloomy exile and migrate to the land of the living. What is more challenging to accept is how these entities are portrayed as being so elegant and magnanimous. Beyond that, how is one to believe that captivating fairy maidens might crave a mortal existence like ours? In foreigners' eyes, a deity is a deity. Paradise is their domain, yet they may occasionally foray outside to perform some benevolent intervention. As far as having deities living in our midst is concerned, that is an phenomenon "made in China". A foreign expert on literature wrote: "In the Chinese novel, senior deities always try to control inferior deities, especially in preventing matrimony between delectable deities and mere mortals."

The second aspect is the figure of the incorrigibly honest man. This type of person is plain in appearance, not precocious and ekes out a pitiful and poor life. His prime merit is his honest simplicity. Suddenly one day, a fairy or fox spirit or snake spirit comes along and tries every means and tramples over every barrier to win his hand in marriage. Foreigners regard this kind of trope as being like a sermon, enshrining Chinese wisdom. They know the tale of how, when you cannot reach a bunch of grapes, you insist they must be sour. On the other hand, they are unfamiliar with the Chinese proverb: "Curb your thirst by staring at the plum."

The third aspect is the poems which precede the narrative of a novel or act as a corollary. One article by a foreign critic reads: "The verse at the beginning of a novel limns its bare outline. This is an embellishment by the publisher. The verse at the end is an ethical appraisal. A discerning reviewer would not pass comment on them." Another article by a foreigner has a crisper ring to it, namely identifying these poems as "the escort and bodyguard of the narrative".

Although ancient novels incorporate many effete habits, they arouse feelings of satisfaction and give the impression of being inimitably Chinese and authentically literary. Tremendous pleasure is to be derived from perusing the letters on the page. Since I love to read these "old things", I sample the remarks others have made about them. Foreigners tend not to pass penetrating judgements owing to the paucity of their background knowledge. Likewise, I have disdain for the essays by so-called "new experts" in China. In the main these flaunt avant-garde theories appropriated from the West. Their articles are laced with half-baked jargon in translation, which prove insipid on the palette. It is on a par with using an imported measuring tape to recreate uniforms from the

Tang Dynasty. At present, so many factories emphasise localisation. The practice of superimposing bogus foreign labels onto domestic products has largely fallen by the wayside. Apparently, in literature there is no comparable trend.

Lately, a retired provincial senior cadre asked me to recommend a few novels and so I purchased a set of "banned" publications for him. This was a hefty, ten-volume collection consisting of dozens of Ming and Qing Dynasty novels. One week later, he told me: "They're good, really good." To his mind: "The novelists of today are pretentious yet bold. They write about what they don't know." He reeled off several of the titles dealing with cracking down on corruption. His remarks were amusing: "The details are pure fiction. Meetings are not conducted like that and backhanders aren't passed around in that way. These writers don't know about the art of officialdom in China." I responded: "The authors themselves are not to blame. When they were sent to work in the provinces, they only served as assistants to the county head. If they had been the vice premier then they would know all there is to know about life."

Wu Cheng'en was awesome. He never tried to delve too deeply into matters with which he was not intimate.

A Lost Quarter Hour of My Life

Everywhere we venture in life we always run into certain faces that can be described as a patchwork of five organs. The attentive eyes are a gift from the bearer's boss. The ears are alert to the sounds of the corridor and the stairwell. The nose is pointed towards the street market outside the window. The mouth and tongue wag with the hearsay of the doorkeeper's office. This kind of person perplexes those around them. Even if we are familiar with them, we often cannot recall their name.

By contrast, Lu Yao's five facial organs belonged purely to himself. They keened in one direction. That was the loneliness and towering pride in his heart. In his brief life, we two spent a quarter of an hour together, during which his five organs became etched on my memory.

Two days ago, a friend called me and asked: "Did you hear the news about Lu Yao?" I told him that I had just received it. The other end of the line fell silent for a while and then sprang to life again. "I recall the sentence you said at the beginning of the year." Months earlier I went to Xi'an to ask Mr Jia Pingwa to compose a piece of fiction to be serialised in our magazine. During that trip I visited Lu Yao on behalf of a friend. When I came back, he asked me how he was. I realised that he wanted to know what Lu Yao was writing. "We only chatted for fifteen minutes." I kept quiet for some time and then added: "I felt that he was shrouded in a grey shadow. That is for certain, but I could not tell what this meant." Now I can explain it clearly. It was the aura of another world and the manifestation of its power. What fragile creatures human beings are! The throbbing heart pounding away, as it was designed to, simply ground to a standstill for no apparent reason. How could this man, Lu Yao, have been allowed to tramp such a short journey?

That day the weather in Xi'an was erratic. A combination of sleet and snow wafted through the air. I rode a bicycle from the guesthouse of Northwest University and reached the Shaanxi Writers Association after zigzagging around for thirty-five minutes. Squeezing through a pinched back gate, I had to negotiate a succession of hairpin bends before reaching his apartment. I tapped lightly at the door. At the sound of footsteps pattering inside I glanced at my wristwatch and the time showed 12:45 PM.

A young lady opened the door. The room was rather dim. I couldn't make out her face and guessed that she must be his daughter. I told her why I was there and she led me into an even dimmer chamber. This was Lu Yao's workshop. When I entered, he had already risen from a single bed. The quilt had been brushed aside. I introduced myself and then apologised: "I'm terribly sorry for interrupting your noontime nap."

His manner was rather affable and he shook my hand and offered me a seat. While pouring water for me, he remarked casually: "I just got up." I originally thought that he was pulling my leg. Later, on reading his diary *When the Morning Starts at Noon*, serialised in *Woman* magazine, I grasped that this was his peculiar lifestyle.

I relayed my friend's greeting to him and enquired about his health. He sat back on the single bed and replied: "You can see for yourself." At the time he was wearing a cardigan and woollen trousers. The room was not just naturally dark; there had been a power-cut. Even though I could sense he was smiling, his face was not fully visible.

In the past, I had read a few of Lu Yao's novels. When *Life* was all the rage, I read the book after having watched the film. Once *Ordinary World* was awarded the Mao Dun Literary Prize, I was itching for a while to devour the whole epic. Every time I gazed at that triple-decker tome, I felt knotted up inside. Since I was not so familiar with his work, I was lost for words. Finding a suitable topic for conversation made the ambience in the room slightly uneasy. As soon as he knew the purpose of my trip to Xi'an, he said: "Pingwa writes faster and his health is also better than mine." Following a pause, he went on: "If the time is convenient, I shall write a piece for your magazine. Lately, I've been sketching the synopsis for a short story. The trouble is that I struggle to keep calm and focused. We can keep in touch through letters." I understood that he was trying to smooth out the atmosphere of unfamiliarity. Even now, I am rather touched by his kindly consideration.

He occupied the bed and I the sofa, two metres apart. I knew he was trying to inject a casual feeling into the air. As he spoke, he looked at me intently. When I was talking, he stared out of the window. The pane was half masked by the curtain. From where we were sitting, it was impossible to tell what was outside. I guess that from the outside one could not see what was inside. A dingy pall seemed to linger beyond the glass. When Lu Yao saw me glancing at the window now and then, he smiled and said: "See, what weather we're having." I knew that this was his way of apologising for the gloomy state of the room. Without thinking, I parroted out: "Yep, what weather."

I read every installment of *When the Morning Starts at Noon*. Even though I felt tired when I finished reading it, this was without fail the first column to which I would turn when a new issue came out. Each time I picked it up, it would bring to mind his appearance as he fixed his eyes on the window. On the publication of the last installment in December 1992, I came face to face with Lu Yao's colour photograph on the front cover of the magazine.

In the late 1980s and early 1990s, two events shocked the Chinese literary world. One was the suicide of the poet Haizi, who laid his head across a railway sleeper in March 1989. The other was the death by hanging of the Taiwanese wayfarer San Mao. These two instances of self-destruction placed much pressure on young folk who aspired to forge a literary career. The passing of Lu Yao no doubt aggravated the strain on people of letters. Of course, Lu Yao is not entirely gone. The significance of his literary achievements will continue to redound through the younger generations who take up his books. And so, the loss of Lu Yao was more potent and gave cause for meditation.

He was a writer born immediately after the founding of the People's Republic of China. In him we can discern many of the hallmarks of contemporary Chinese authors. When I came to the thirty-eighth section of the series *When the Morning Starts at Noon*, my heart seemed as though it was weighing me down. That was in September, just two months before the lamentable news of his demise was broadcast. In the later chapters of the serial he examined in detail the process of how he revised the second draft of *An Ordinary World*. He was struck by illness, clawed his way to recovery and then sprinted towards completion. Poring over this today, we can identify how he stumbled in the course of his last struggle. He sank into performing "the natural duty of a writer". At the same time, he set down on paper how he received all manner of support and succour from people in every walk of life. One of the catalysts for finishing the project was his need to repay all the concern that had been bestowed on him.

As I read these words I pondered how for a time after the founding of the New China, writers were ostensibly the beloved and coddled children of our society (one of the characteristics of this era has been the great importance attached to literature). During the Cultural Revolution, these coddled children were subject to draconian discipline and abruptly weaned. Afterwards, they were given an excessive transfusion of blood.

Authors have occupied an integral position in China and thus have developed a grotesque trait. They are unwilling to allow themselves to be left out in the cold and have no tolerance for such a situation. Among the present waves of Reform and Opening-up, when can a writer truly have a free hand to produce whatever he or she likes? To put this another way, it is better that writers are forsaken by society and learn to be self-sufficient. If the literary world mirrored the system of responsibility in the countryside, there would be policies to be implemented and various forms of concern and guidance to support them. The writers could inhabit their own sphere of responsibility and be at ease. They would be sure to cultivate their crops as prudently as farmers do.

That day when I bade farewell to Lu Yao, it was one o'clock on the dot. The borrowed digital watch on my wrist broke out into a nauseating chime. Lu Yao smiled and asked: "Why do you wear a thing like that?" I answered with a grin: "These days in Xi'an I've felt very lonely." At the moment of writing, I miss the jingle jangle of that cheap timepiece. It is a pity that I long ago returned it to its owner.

Written in 1992

Tie Ning in Close-up

Tie Ning is the kind of writer who never rests on her laurels. In her recent novels and prose she has gradually refined her depiction of female characters into a kind of crystalline and lustrous texture. This feeling struck me as I read the novels *The Rose Gate* (1990), *Octday* (1992), and the prose collection *The White Night of Women* (1992). In the 1920s and 1930s, the main trend in depicting women's problems was "Ibsen's Nora goes out". What shocked the eardrums of the establishment was the assertion that women were no longer naught.

Now, the page has been turned on that florid style of dramatisation. Some writers are still interested in the predicament of "women going out to work" or the implications of "women are no longer naught". They lag behind the times. Tie Ning's invaluable contribution lies in her efforts to describe "what a woman is" through her literary images. Although the idea is not constructed in such a way that the scaffolding is obvious, the architecture is definitely conspicuous. In a recent conversation with Tie Ning about her creative work, I used a particular phrase: "Nora should have a home of her own."

To build a healthy, just and positive idea of the feminine falls within the scope of cultural history. Actually, seventy years have elapsed since the emergence of the concept of the "new woman". Nevertheless, we have not advanced so very far in our understanding of the theory. Here I absolutely refute the suggestion that Tie Ning is a feminist (she is only a brilliant writer). All the same, her literary praxis glistens with an unconscious light. In truth, the whole of society has the responsibility to contemplate the question of gender. It should not only be the preserve of writers, let alone women writers. Tie Ning's female protagonists are not intentionally characterised as outstanding or exemplary, yet she reveals their better qualities by digging deep. In this respect her protagonists are neither mighty nor exalted, but candid, natural and sincere throughout their tribulations.

In Tie Ning's new works, apart from retaining her established style, with its tranquillity, self-sufficiency, capacity to provoke thought, and measured sensitivity, she has infused a perspective that combines a fresh energy with concrete reality. The themes of her work in this period can be summarised as: the hardship of ascending from the bottom, emotional disjunction, loneliness, and love and hate in their broadest sense. Her creative thinking is singular, simple and forceful, especially in her novels. She does not grandstand her prodigious talents as many other writers do. Instead she possesses a peerless sense of system and far-reaching insight. Her novels are akin to an underground river. You cannot see the water with the naked eye. Still, from the variety of crops and shining green leaves sprouting from the earth above, you can detect the quality and abundance of the clear spring.

The other vital dimension to Tie Ning's work is how she never leaves her readers or the critical circle feeling disheartened.

Recently, during the Spring Festival, I read her novel *Stupid Flower*. I was in raptures and could not bear to put it down. I selected one portion of it to publish in our prose magazine. I do not know whether this was an act of violation to the work. My belief is that as far as art is concerned, the devil is in the detail. Take the Xi'an city wall as an example. Its perimeter measures 13.74 kilometres, representing a corridor suspended in the air. To be exact, it has 98 gate-towers, four corner towers, one Scholar's Tower, 598 apertures, ten tracks by which horses can mount the wall, and 178 drainage channels. If you just discuss each detail in isolation, it does not comprise a city wall. The grandeur of the edifice lies in how every minutiae is there to be examined at close range.

Through the modish media of smartphone messaging, I sent my observation on her novel to Tie Ning, requesting her reaction. Her answer was encouraging: "Follow your own tack. I too agree with this idea. This makes me sound immodest. The paragraph about the dusk happens to be a favourite of mine."

A Pair of Straw Sandals

The history of the USA stretches back barely two centuries, so Americans regard "old things" with serious eyes for much the same reason as the Chinese are fond of ancient antiquities. What is more, they invest "old things" with human emotions. In April 1990, a man named Mitchell (Clark Mitchell, Director of the American Studies Center at Princeton University and an eminent expert in the field of Comparative Literature) related a story to me. An American writer wanted to change his job, but he found it hard to part with his typewriter. He stood on the street and tried to palm off the contraption onto somebody else. A sign alongside him declared: "Used, only $11!" An Asian passerby tried to haggle him down to $10. The writer shook his head with sadness and replied: "My hands have been hammering away at this for eleven years. It really is an heirloom." When the Asian man returned, having been around the block, he found that the writer was gone. The typewriter lay dumped at the foot of the wall. He picked it up and went away contentedly.

Mr Mitchell is a first-class contemporary American scholar. In January 1990, he came to Northwest University in Xi'an to attend the Sino-American Symposium on Comparative Literature. I was invited to recite one of my newly-composed poems at this event.

Space

The prepossession of the grazing flock
Left the shepherd with a lull
To finely hew the haft of his crop.

The tent stood leagues from the river
Those shallows did not scintillate.
The complexion of the tent and grass
Offered no clues as to which was older.

A ewe became mesmerised by the bank opposite
Though was oblivious
As to what might await her
Should she decamp over yonder.

Her scheme was foiled, so she was made to bear
The full force of the burnished whip.
Her torso and hefty bobtail
Smarted more than bleats could tell.

When she arrived under the pall of night,
To her astonishment, she found
The currents in fact were a source of propulsion.

The drover intercepted her
Lividly upon the mead
And rewarded her boldness with a hiding.

> After daybreak he, unrelenting,
> Pitched his old tent once again
> Over the homemade carnage
> On the riverside.

Summer 1989

The piece left a deep impression on Mr Mitchell and we had further discussions about it after the meeting. He knew very little about mainstream modern Chinese poetry. What knowledge he had did not extend beyond the 1980s. He was familiar with Bei Dao and Shu Ting. I brought him up to speed about a number of promising young poets, including Ling Mang, Wang Jiaqing and Zhou Jingzi from Beijing, Yu Jian from Yunnan, and Han Dong from Nanjing, together with other experimental writers like Sun Wenbo and Yang Ran from Sichuan. He then vowed that he would introduce these newcomers to American readers. It was a pity that, at the time, I had few materials readily to hand.

We also shared our thoughts on older American poets such as Robert Bly and the winner of the 1989 Pulitzer Prize, Richard Wilbur. He was startled to learn how popular American poets were with Chinese readers. To his mind, "the field of Chinese literature is a sealed old box". I told him that *Poetry Magazine* and *Divine Poetry* have thousands upon thousands of subscribers. He shrugged his shoulders and mused: "It seems that I am the one who has come here from a tiny country." When I gave him a signed copy of my newly-printed commentary on the poet Xi Murong, I told him that it was from an edition of 40,000. He responded frankly that: "In the US this would have made you an absolute killing."

Before he returned to the United States, I gave him a pair of straw sandals. They were new, but the straw they were fashioned from had been treated with smoke so as simulate the appearance of age. This was a souvenir I bought at Mount Emei. I instructed him on how to wear them, adding: "Fifty years ago, Mao Zedong and his comrades in arms trod the entire Long March with these on their feet. The famous journalist from your country Harrison Salisbury put down a vivid description of this in his book."

He was delighted and even somewhat moved. "I shall be sure to cherish them. Did Salisbury himself wear this same kind?"

"I guess he wouldn't have. He was too old for them, but I'm sure he was familiar with shoes of this ilk."

"Then I shall become more famous than him. I've brought back the choicest relic from the People's Republic of China."

My Two Legs Can Surely Outpace the Chinese

Bill Holm was forty-two years old, six feet five inches tall, weighed more than 240 pounds and was of Icelandic descent. His hair and the beard that circumnavigated his face were auburn. He was a contemporary American poet and musician. At one of the meetings held at Southwest University in Minnesota, the president asked who would like to be seconded to teach at Xi'an Jiaotong University. As soon as those words left his mouth, this hulking fellow raised a stout hand. Another professor alongside him whispered: "China is so backward. We've consigned all our cow-drawn carts and iron ploughs to museums. They still sell and use them. The worst thing is that you can't drive around, only walk." Bill Holm mulled this over for a while and then answered: "My two Icelandic legs can surely outpace the Chinese."

In September 1986, his Pan Am flight landed in Beijing and he was itching to reach the ancient city of Xi'an and enter the gate of Jiaotong University. It appeared that the school was even more anxiously awaiting him. The second he entered the campus hotel the staff at the Foreign Languages Department sent him the curriculum timetable. He was supposed to teach British and American Literature to two grades of graduate students. Simultaneously, he was to serve as the language instructor to a class of "trainee teachers".

Bill Holm had a sardonic eye and described his students as: "The victims of the chaotic and inadequate universities of cultural-revolution days. The students varied in age from nineteen to their mid-forties and came from the far corners: Xinjiang, Qinghai, Hunan, Manchuria, Suzhou. Some had Chinese accents so exotic they were forced to speak to their classmates in English most of the time."

He was taken aback by the students' knowledge and their study ethic. He conceded in all honesty that they had a quality lacking in most modern American students; that is to say, their zeal for learning. Deeply moved as he was by their dedication, he always worked overtime and savoured every second in their company. Even at midday in the summer months, he would make himself available to answer students' questions.

He launched a very effective programme of teaching reform. Soon after the semester began, he realised that passivity was the norm in Chinese classrooms. He then compiled an elementary textbook of his own design, selecting some of the masterpieces from the *Norton Anthology of Literature*. In class, he discussed the authors' creative intentions and their artistic techniques. His manner of teaching not only enlivened the atmosphere in the classroom but also deepened the emotional engagement between teachers and students. A year later, when he was about to leave for the US, many of the older students even shed tears. Back in his homeland, he continued enthusiastically to nurture the students by mailing them books and reading materials. Furthermore, he helped to arrange for a number of them to study in America.

Bill Holm loved to drink Qingdao beer and smoke Phoenix cigarettes. It was such a pity that he seldom had the chance to do the former. He preferred Phoenix cigarettes for their "chocolaty" taste. I asked him how he felt about Chinese chocolate. He shrugged his broad shoulders and said "tasty". I told him: "Phoenix cigarettes were the name brand during the time of Mao Zedong and so were tricky to obtain back then. Nowadays, they are ten a penny on the market." He showed a great interest in this. "Your comment made me love them even more. I admire Chairman Mao very much. He was a great farmer-cum-statesman."

As a scholar and one of the important contemporary US poets, during his year in China he was able to visit a welter of destinations. He trekked around noteworthy historical remains and trod the main streets and alleys to glean a thorough understanding of the country. After returning home, he toured countless cities to share his feelings about the Reform and Opening-up. In 1990, he published a book entitled *Coming Home Crazy*, which expressed his observations. The language of the work is humorous and the viewpoint novel and thought-provoking. He both praised and criticised the situation in China, putting forth an objective survey of the land through the eyes of foreigners. The book caused a stir.

Bill Holm loved China. He adored the ancient culture and admired the present-day reforms. In the most recent letter I received from him, he wrote: "I shall come back to China again. I'll once more stomp the main streets and alleys and meet my old friends. This time I shall be sure to imbibe some fresh and unexpected experiences. My two Icelandic legs believe that more than I do myself."

Lonesome to the Limit:
A Cautionary Tale from the 1990s

Picture this: you are inching along a narrow, interminable corridor; pitch dark without any window or light. You cannot make out a thing. Your twitching ears can detect your own anxious breath without any clue about where the end will be. The corridor goes on forever and turning back is out of the question. You forget where the entrance is located. This is being lonesome to the limit. No one can traverse this desert of the spirit. Not even lower animals, well-accustomed to migrating individually can negotiate the situation. Wolves may howl from the depths of a wild land.

One Sunday afternoon, twenty-eight-year-old Marcy was struck by this strain of loneliness. She hailed from a university in Minnesota. In her hometown, she was used to rich and vibrant spare-time activities. She swam, went skating, attended concerts or drove around for pleasure. All this changed when she moved over to lecture in Xi'an. There was no skating rink in Shaanxi; her designer skates sat around inside the cupboard like a work of art. She complained about the lack of decent concerts and how she had never learned to ride a bicycle. She fed cassette after cassette of ancient Chinese music into the recorder, but the natural and lyrical string music gave her the sensation of dangling in mid-air. What is more, it sent a shiver through her mind, resulting in a forlorn melancholy. Having no other choice, she called friends at home and abroad, beseeching them for books.

Modern Americans seldom seem to read books. In the

ever-changing epoch of IT, they have no time to digest tomes. They can forage whatever they need from the newspapers and now the internet. That is why the US mass media industry thrives. Marcy later reflected that: "My China trip turned me into a scholar of the last century. At weekends and on Sunday mornings I'd always wedge my head into weighty volumes, trying to digest archaic knowledge."

One gloomy Sunday afternoon in May, Marcy's lonesomeness reached its nadir. For consecutive days, the once animate clouds found themselves becalmed on the Qinling Mountains. Dark mists jammed the air above Xi'an. It appeared as if rain was imminent, though it never materialised. It appeared as if the clouds were about to shunt away, but they stayed stationery. When she felt her breath becoming really jagged, she went outside. An hour later she found a bedraggled madwoman at the corner of a road on Southern University Avenue. She brought her back to her room at the foreign experts' hotel and assisted her in taking a shower, combing her hair and dressing her in fresh clothes. She warbled songs and grilled Welsh rarebit for her. After the woman had eaten her fill, she broke into hysterics, battering the TV set, the mirror and cupboard. She even flayed Marcy's clothes into strips before slipping out without a word.

After surviving this catastrophe, Marcy explained what had happened to the hotel staff. She admitted in all honesty that: "She had every reason to go berserk. My motives for bringing her back here were selfish. I did it to lift my own spirits. I'll foot the bill for repairs."

"My spare time is a void," Marcy added irritably. "I can't be like my Chinese colleagues and channel all my heart and mind into the job. It's impossible for me. I am a living, breathing woman. I can't swank about those luxury hotels where they provide entertainment for Westerners. I'm not wealthy enough. The standard of service on offer there is not the same as back home. And yet the fees they charge are equally steep. I think the Chinese Bureau of Education should take into account the lot of 'paupers' like us."

Marcy was indeed not an affluent soul. I know of another teacher in a different university, a Briton by the name of Charles Watt. Twice a month he would fly to Guangzhou for the weekend and take the train to Hong Kong, then fly home punctually on Monday morning. Charles's family had two enterprises down there and they covered all of his expenses. On top of that, they supplied him with credit cards to use in the two international hotels in Xi'an. In his spare time, he typically stayed in a hotel and whenever lessons came around he would cruise to the classroom by taxi.

Now Marcy has already gone back to the States. In her last letter to me, she wrote: "I miss so many old friends and places in China. I've kept up the pastimes of Chinese classical music and poetry. I've even found it hard to break back into American leisure pursuits. China is a huge magnet. Very big and very good too."

The Country Bumpkin: Early Reflections on Jia Pingwa

By country bumpkin I am not suggesting poverty, backwardness, narrow-mindedness or conservatism. This word describes his inner soul, denoting simplicity, depth, a lack of ostentation, and an ordered and systematic mien. To be more explicit, I am not referring to the firewood of a farming household, but the kitchen smoke winding and rising above the rooftop after the fuel has been totally consumed. Reading Jia Pingwa's works will not change your viewpoints immediately. It is as if he is conversing with you. He never deigns to correct you, listening instead in silence. Then he will pass his comment calmly. This will be neither sharp nor barbed. Still it should have a rinsing effect on your way of thinking and warm your attitude. In the countryside, the kitchen smoke in the dusk represents an atmosphere that can console a man's heart like no other.

To be frank, among Jia Pingwa's work I love his prose best of all. As far as his novels are concerned, I am fonder of the atmosphere behind the stories. It is just like when I face a tree. No matter how grand, how stately or grotesque that might be, I always try to imagine the shape of its roots (I dislike those plants which have roots exposed above the ground) as well as how it interacts with the soil. In this way, my mind's eye never runs short of spectacles on which to feast.

The relationship between life and literary creation should proceed as follows. We should not comprehend "experiencing life" as "moving in and squatting somewhere for a while". We should look around and search for "materials". We should not burrow away at the corners of a wall, nor should we poke about virgin roots foraging for "aesthetically-shaped nodes". We should not try to retrieve experiences seen vicariously and display them as something rare on the walls of our houses.

As a brilliant author, Jia Pingwa's uniqueness is to be found in his spiritual home, which is so richly endowed by nature. Shangzhou Prefecture furnishes him with both his physical and artistic life. Shangzhou is the base camp of his creation. His spiritual roots are firmly anchored there. As he says in the preface to his novel Turbulence: "The Shangzhou I write about is not the Shangzhou marked on the administrative map. It is my fictional land, a conduit for Shangzhou and the Shangzhou in my heart."

So many comments have been published on Jia Pingwa, a fair number of them critical. Admirers and detractors, however, share one common thread. That is, none among all the other contemporary Chinese writers can be said to possess a spiritual homeland with such a broad, rich, and animated nature. No other current Chinese literary works evoke such an affinity with the land, the river and its tributaries, the hills and their undulating terrain, or are able to distinguish the texture of various rocks and notice how trees intertwine with each other. Even when an "official road" is rerouted, he can describe an appreciable difference in ambience. There is no formula or system behind his basic vocabulary. Almost every piece by him has its own peculiar narration. Once you immerse your head in his works, you will smell the pungent, slowly-rising smell of the forest undergrowth, you will glimpse the criss-crossing grain of the rocks, you will hear the water purling along the river from its banks, and even the tiny craters in a whirlpool become vivid before your eyes and discernible to the ears. He is all too familiar with this ancient patch of land. He knows the mountains, waters, rocks, and trees, as well as the traditional folk customs. He used twenty years to taste and absorb the inner links between these components (until he reached the age of forty). I am sure that he still dare not claim that he understands his homeland and will continue to masticate while the scenery of rivers and mountains not yet utilised comes into sharper view.

Among the dozens of books he has published, the most striking characteristic is his repeated cogitation over human nature and the physical environment of his native area. Each repetition adds an extra layer of clarity. He is just like William Faulkner who never ventured beyond Yoknapatawapha County in his stories and yet managed to eschew both monotony and verbosity. The creative process is comparable to the formation of a road. It is necessary for different men's feet to tread back and forth endlessly, so a conspicuous track will be cleaved across the wild land. As a fellow from the countryside, the contrast between the Jia Pingwa of today and the Jia Pingwa of twenty years ago is that his feet are not only planted on that ancient land, but he has also sprouted wings to soar high in the air.

On 21st February (according to the Lunar Calendar) 1952, Jia Pingwa was born into a well-off farming family in Jinpeng Hamlet, Danfeng County, located in the south of Shaanxi Province. "The Jia clan was a leading local family. It had more than twenty members. His father ranked fourth among the sons and his three elder brothers had many offspring between them." Among the younger generation, Jia Pingwa ranked eighth. Although he was born in the countryside, he was not strictly speaking a son of the soil. His father Jia Yanchun worked as a primary school teacher and his devouring of the Confucian Classics cast a strong shadow over his heart and soul alike. Readers can find ample evidence of this in his essay "In Memory of My Father", written on the occasion of him succumbing to cancer.

Shaanxi is very mysterious and elusive. These features are more pronounced in the south of the province (northern Shaanxi is relatively impoverished. It only experienced a brief period of prosperity after the Red Army arrived in 1935). There are such descriptions in Jia Pingwa's novels (for example, his novel *Turbulence*). *The Mystery of Jia Pingwa* by Sun Jianxi states: "One street adjoins three provinces – to the south is Hubei, to the east is Henan and to the north is Shaanxi. At the centre of the street crouches a dark rock, which marks the axis between the three. There is a trio of shops on the street. The door of each bears the name of the province to which it belongs and each specialises in selling named local products from that place." All of the characters in Jia Pingwa's works are endowed with soul and this radiates out through their faces. It is the land that has bred them that nourishes this feature. As a result, in the critical world, one viewpoint states that Mr Jia's creations belong to the category of the "cultural novel". That is not an entirely accurate estimation, though there is a grain of truth in it.

Jia Pingwa's attitude towards this "mystery" is blunt and direct. He narrates events which defy ready description with an easy and calm heart. His inner heart is at ease, having been tempered by its own dormant power. Whereas other writers employ mysterious techniques to handle mysterious subjects (such as authors who devote themselves to *qigong* or life on the Tibetan Plateau), he does not conform to that pattern. We could praise him by quoting Hemingway's words from *Death in the Afternoon*: "If he mystifies to avoid a straight statement, which is very different from breaking so-called rules of syntax or grammar to make an effect which can be obtained in no other way, the writer takes a longer time to be known as a fake and other writers who are afflicted by the same necessity will praise him in their own defense. True mysticism should not be confused with incompetence in writing which seeks to mystify where there is no mystery but is really only the necessity to fake to cover lack of knowledge or the inability to state clearly. Mysticism implies a mystery and there are many mysteries; but incompetence is not one of them, nor is overwritten journalism made literature by the injection of a false epic quality. Remember this too: all bad writers are in love with epic."

Jia Pingwa has displayed his inimitable quality in disinterring "folk customs and tales". In his novels, the traditional "hardcore" has been dissolved like particles of ink which, by dripping one-by-one into a bucket, actually makes the water more transparent. His novels together with his prose have become mellower in tone, broader in their reach and more piquant. This is down to the percolation of the ink.

Without prevarication, I must admit that I have my reservations about his criteria for selecting tales involving folk customs and local proverbs. In 1992, I wrote an article to voice this concern. I am less keen on his works involving the supernatural and spirits, such as those found in his *Chronicles of Mount Taibai*. His pen sometimes fixates upon gods and ghosts. These pieces which quest after the unexplained emit a haunting, hellish temper which tenses the spine. True enough, a writer's characteristics are derived from how they project the image of the human heart and what is imagined therein. Nonetheless, nightmarish and sick images can serve to disfigure that original integrity.

I even hazarded a guess that, had Mr Jia achieved fame later on, had his path to success been steeper or had he received less flattery and fewer jaded reviews, he might have developed greater patience and refinement in his choice of themes and materials. Jia Pingwa is a prolific writer. Most of his works concern Shangzhou. However, his present creations lack a sense of large-scale systematic unity. His *Shangzhou Series* is not regimented with a careful continuity in mind. It appears that he is disinterested in the pull of history. The majority of his energies are diffused among ethics and background. Actually, his Shangzhou could be very discrete, like Faulkner's Yoknapatawapha. "I didn't image that the world I created would serve as the cornerstone to the whole universe. Small as that cornerstone might be, once it is dislodged the universe will come crashing down."

When I was in the process of finishing this article, we shared yet another telephone conversation. He told me he had just returned from Yao County. His voice was exuberant and resonant. I know that he visited the local reservoir there to further his new novel. When I asked about how it was progressing, he answered in a strong Shaanxi burr: "If you have time, come over for a peek. This one is nothing like anything I've done before."

October 1992

A Response from Mu Tao

2nd August 1996

Dear Jia,

I have just finished reading your manuscript. I really appreciate you entrusting this to me and seeking my feedback.

During the process of reading, some ideas occurred to me. They accumulated like residue on the insides of a boiling pot. Whether it is with our heads raised high or our faces hanging down, we encounter each other virtually every day. Talking in person is not always as efficacious as expressing one's self in writing. Our tongues never really keep pace with the rapidity of our thoughts, so I thought that craning over a page was the best position in which to clearly record my reactions.

I have read through the manuscript twice. First, I read it sequentially, being attentive to any aspect which did not flow smoothly, as well as being mindful of any echoes of your previous writings. Only then did I focus on close reading the characters, the plot and the interconnection between finer details. My aim was to discern how these minutiae functioned within the novel. The anxieties I thought were in my heart prior to reading proved illusory or insignificant. I wasn't reading with the eye of an editor or a critic, but from the standpoint of an ordinary reader. I tried to read objectively. You know, this is rather challenging. As one who is familiar with both your work and your daily life, certain obstacles are encountered. To be frank, the novel for the most part left me jolted. You have recast your former style in so many respects. Some of the more delicate parts I found touching. It was as though the finesse and patination of your extant writing had been rarefied. Other places irked me and the compulsion to share this with you forms a further reason for this letter.

If a writer doesn't expose and criticise human backwardness and ignorance, he forfeits the chance to be upheld as a distinguished author to whom are attributed words like "foresight" and "sagacity". At the same time, every literary master is protective of, and steadily nurtures, the garden found in his innermost heart. On the surface, this sounds contradictory, and yet these opposites are in fact a perfect reflection of one another, their glorious sunlight too being mirrored. I appreciate the motif of this novel very much, for it conveys the sensation of crossing a threshold. The urbanisation of a community – Benevolent Lenient Village – on the hinterland between the country and the city is recounted. What sets the village apart from ordinary rural settlements are its vestiges of history, namely relics from the Ming Dynasty which were nourished by the cultural atmosphere of the West Guanzhong Academy in the Qing era. Thus, we may regard it as a capsule of how Chinese society developed from ancient times into its modern incarnation.

The farmland in the suburbs has been commandeered by the government. The modern city, which changes by the day, stridently advances towards the last bastion of farming life – countryside dwellings. One party wishes to be relocated and the other is determined to stay put. The uniqueness of the novel lies in how the reactionary cause is rendered as a positive force. You explore their just and flagrant efforts at resistance, their struggle, their beleaguered situation, and their total decimation. What shocked me most was the vivid description of the collapse of the final remnants of the perimeter walls of the academy.

The novel penetrates x-ray-like into the psychological struggle of every villager. Having been divested of their land, these farmers on the fringes lose their original pallor. They are yet to forge a new identity for themselves. Society pushes them to its margins or, to use the current vernacular, they are reduced to "jobbing hands". Gone is their land and normal professions. They are either chaff, surplus to the requirements of society, or else excess baggage weighing down its back. In order to survive or to retain their dignity, they toil away, becoming nomads at the edges of the earth like Chivalry, or try to ape the city-dwellers like Old Ran, or leech off others like Brow. The majority of them become peddlers on tricycles, hawking vegetables and other goods along the roadsides and lanes. Food and clothing cause them no worries. What catches in their craws is that there is nowhere for their souls to recline. In order to safeguard the last "root" of the village they go so far as to build a model cemetery with mausoleum space for the living.

The fine threads represented by Chivalry, Grandpa Cloud Forest and the narrator of the novel form a futile net, trying to offer up resistance. The purpose of the net is very simple – oppose relocation and protect their homes. They are somewhat reminiscent of the queue-sporting battalions of General Zhang Xiong, who sought to restore the Qing monarchy. A group of people take direct action on behalf of the reactionary cause, with a kind of rancid, sorrowful nobility resonating from the beginning to the end. Although these folks were nursed by a scholarly atmosphere, they are farmers by inclination. Circumscribed by their own natural conditions, the development they so long for remains unrealised. They are marooned at the stage of mimicry and copying others.

Chivalry is a vibrant character in the novel. His behaviour embodies the spirit of a peasant uprising. He takes rashness as bravery and hooliganism as righteous indignation. His ultimate fate also typifies what happens to rebels in the long river of Chinese history (there are plenty of instances of farmers like this). I happen to think that the value of the novel is to be found in its double-layered criticism. It scrutinises the backwardness and ignorance of farmers and the unhealthy elements in urban civilisation – namely the bypassing of human sensitivities, development at any cost and by every means, and the mob mentality (as witnessed in the football riot).

The novel is structured like a snowball. It begins from something slight but tactile, and swells to embody the developmental process of urban civilisation. Unlike some other writers, you haven't taken an entrepreneur or a big company as your subject, describing the current of reform as being like a set of banking waves. That kind of panoramic style is not your forte. You imply that adopting such an approach hinders the author from reaching into the pulsating heart of a culture. If one is not careful enough, it is easy to end up composing something superficial. And yet, you have cleverly chosen to trace the resilience of a village in the suburbs and dramatise the entire process from resistance, through hesitation to helpless resignation. You have thoroughly examined the incontrovertible pattern to be found in an industrialising society. The underlying meaning is exposed through the pains and hardship endured as civilisation progresses step-by-step.

In addition, I noticed how in this novel you ventriloquise a paragraph from one of my articles through the mouth of a character. Thank you for concurring with me on how to understand the trend of human civilisation. In history, the idea of farmers advancing is usually ignored. We belong to a sprawling agricultural nation, but there is a tendency to generalise about "petty farmers". Farmers may be mere grains of sands, but collectively they form the Gobi Desert.

Today, unprecedented change is simmering in the Chinese countryside. First comes the swift uprising of the entrepreneurs in the counties and the towns. Then follows the city-ward surge of migrant workers. The change sweeps through like a blustering storm, leaving large and middle-sized cities perplexed. Historically, the peasant uprisings originated with Chen Sheng and Wu Guang (third century BC). They fought to secure a basic livelihood, including land to farm. Even after the founding of the People's Republic of China, the "people's commune" movement floundered because the government confiscated the land from the farmers and reneged on their promises. Accordingly, in 1979 the state again implemented the policy of "when the sheep have gone the fences will still be mended", returning the land to the farmers. Now, the farmers have begun to voluntarily relinquish their land.

The cruel reality tells us that the flesh and blood relationship between farmers and the land has become diluted. Farmers dare not pin all of their hopes on the land. This huge group has hauled their backbone up from the earth and tried to join the principal current of society. Your novel does not portray this situation with such great clarity. Some of the choicer ideas should be described in the course of the narration rather than through images.

There is an obvious change in the use of vocabulary in this novel compared with your previous works. Formerly, you employed the method of line-drawing; direct description without hints of what is to come next or setting up too many lateral branches. The heart is simultaneously moved by emotion and everything springs from the bottom of the heart. The outgrowing of language in this novel, particularly in the activities of the characters and the tone of their conversations, seemingly deploys the technique of stream of consciousness. For example, when people are talking you capture more about the scenery and environment around them. This appears rather miscellaneous, though I feel that this makes the characters appear more vital.

I once read an ancient novel – one from the early Song or Yuan Dynasty. The title escapes me. What I do recall from it was a poetic description, actually the words of a scholar to a comely middle-aged lady:

Steady is the tread of half worn-out shoes;
A mended paper fan wafts with more comfort.
Mellower is the wine cellared for one year;
A pheasant with a longer tail is the head of the nye.
Frisky is the flame of a dying wick;
A beauty in her middle years provides the best consort.

This type of description is exceedingly fine, like a butterfly encircling a blossom and periodically dipping down onto the petals. One of the obvious disadvantages of novels written in Modern Chinese is that they are somewhat facile and slight. A number try to imitate the tenor of European novels in translation. Words strafe the readers, though the connotation is insipid. Others try to emulate the Chinese Classics, being "half-ink and half-water". The novelists in our country devote more energy to style than language. This can be counted as one of the major embarrassments of the Chinese novel.

As I have read your works unrelentingly, one dimension which makes me a little uneasy is your stolid belief in the "miraculous". You positively immerse yourself in this. Tangible traces of the supernatural linger through this novel as well. For example, there are the episodes where Plum's soul migrates out of her body, and where Grandpa Forest Cloud treats diseases. I maintain that aspirations and their auguries appear spontaneously. If a composer works on his score while his thoughts are stymied, he will become enveloped in a melancholy gloom. At this moment, should a leaf happen to fall on his shoulder, his muse may be awakened and the melodies gush forth. This is the supernatural power of aspiration.

The omens of the heavens and the skies are mysterious, but there are hidden reasons behind their appearance. When a storm is brewing, ants might swarm to a different home, snakes slither out of their holes, and startled swallows fly closer to the ground. Or, when an earthquake is about to strike, rats surge onto the streets and chickens and dogs become agitated. I too believe that if you dream about stepping in manure, the next day good fortune will likely come your way. If, on the other hand, it is silver dollars and gold doubloons which pave the ground and cause your soles to ache, daybreak will bring disaster. Money is one of the unfathomable forces in our lives. At times, we treat it as manure, at times we associate it with a fall, or it can even signify the status quo. Only a cigarette paper separates the dream from the waking reality. A peasant awakening from a period of derangement to find that he has the gift of healing does not ring true for me.

When I was a child, my mother spent years indisposed by renal disease. My earliest memory is of my father and elder siblings escorting her to hospital. We visited almost all the clinics close to our home before trying the bigger places in Beijing and Tianjin. After returning home, everyone felt hopeless and she would prostrate herself in the bedroom all day long. One day, with the assistance of a kindhearted neighbour, my father travelled hundreds of miles to invite over a medicine man from the depths of the mountains. He was a lanky fellow with an ashen face, who sat in the chair with the kind of expression that could drive onlookers a thousand miles in repulsion. His medicine was a half-and-half mixture of herbs and seeds, which he doled out handful-by-handful from a tattered cloth bag. He tipped the stuff into a dark jar and then took out a bowl from his bag. He filled the bowl with cold water and swayed it under the lamp while murmuring some incantation. After repeating the process for more than an hour, the jar was full of fluid, which he placed atop the stove to boil. He lit some incense and, once the process was over, retook his seat. When my father humbly made a short query, he would answer it concisely. If barracked with ten enquiries, he might remain silent.

On sipping his concoction, my mother unexpectedly rallied and was able to walk as long as she had one hand steering her along the bedside. This served like a shot in the arm for all concerned and, from then on, the faces of every generation shone with hope. The next day the medicine man departed with ten thousand thanks and as much money as we could cadge to pay him. A fortnight later, my mother passed away and nobody ever mentioned the quack again. Whenever I think about it, I always wonder how my mother, bedridden as she had been for two months, could regain her mobility overnight. Was it the potency of the herbs or had her survival instinct been kick-started? As I have grown older, I increasingly believe that it was the latter.

By the way, in your previous novels you tried your utmost to describe female characters. Under your pen, they are rendered beautiful in their standing postures. Their beauty resides in their poetic temperament, their magnanimity, their grace and charm, even in certain rather inscrutable qualities. After all, the sibyls in your work are bound to be as numerous as those in your imagination. Nonetheless, in this novel you appear to have become rather absentminded. The two female characters are not quite as rounded as their male counterparts. I do not know what you were driving at.

I let my train of thought direct this letter. It is just a casual jotting. You are an established man of letters. I am as clumsy as a cow trying to discuss piano playing with Beethoven. Do not vex yourself over whether I am near to the mark or far from it. Above all, turn a deaf ear if I am mistaken.

> Best regards,
> With my pen's blessing,
> Mu Tao.

Positions and Ideas

It is ridiculous to try and blow out an electric lightbulb as one would a candle. The absurdity lies not in the method but in the underlying idea. Bin Laden was a dangerous individual. His very existence posed a covert threat, yet within al Qaeda he was lauded as a righteous figurehead. We survey this situation from contrary positions – that is where the discrepancy lies.

First, let us talk about positions.

Looking at a cup, the angle of the sides are of little consequence. The volume of the vessel may be ascertained in a single glance. Looking at a detached house, the angles are extremely significant. Studying it from the front or from the back are two different matters. If one climbs the tree at the front of the property to find a new vantage point that is another story too. The place where the observer chooses to stand determines their view.

Looking at the mountains is not at all like looking at a river. The mountains are inanimate, their appearance fluctuating with the rhythm of the year. The river is in perpetual motion, experiencing only minor seasonal variations. Rivers in the north freeze during the winter, but this is only a surface phenomenon. Considering a single mountain, there is a distinction between viewing it from the summit and viewing it from the base. Mountaineers and travellers from afar also have contrasting attitudes towards such an eminence. Fish are the travellers in the water, but they are the kinsmen of the river. Their predilection for the waterway is not the same as that of spectators on the bank. Mighty rivers are different when observed from a horizontal or a vertical angle. They are more different still when seen from their downstream and their backflow. Confucius commented that: "The passage of time is but like the flow of waters, which perseveres day and night." As trite as that saying has now become, it nonetheless calls to mind the loftiness and barrenness of the accumulated sediments of history.

Next, let us talk about ideas.

Ideas are alive. They alter according to current events. Dead ideas are called "conceptions". Advanced ideas are upheld as good ideas. Ideas that fall behind the times are labelled as "outdated". Those who are willing to take the lead drive the vanguard of change. Those bringing up the rear fall into line with these changes, or to use a better term, they respond to them.

Hitherto, the land was the fundamental element of the populace's existence. Land was the basic frame of reference by which a family or the values of a race were judged. Distinctions between large families, rich families, and broken families were determined by the extent of their land ownership. Generals and ministers had lands granted to them by the emperor. They plied their power to obtain further acreage and expand their circle of influence. Shrewd businessmen are apt to try and monopolise the land in the countryside. Those who have land are called "landlords", whereas those who till and tend on behalf of others are called "farmers". Being a farmer is not a profession. Rather, it is the pronoun which embodies that person's identity, just as in ancient times we rendered government officials "lords". Imbalance in land ownership is the basic catalyst for social instability and turbulence. When farmers have no means by which to live "rebellions will be on the rise".

In days of yore, the core values were formulated around agricultural thought and the farm economy.

There is an ancient couplet: "First class citizens, faithful ministers and filial sons / Two major concerns – reading books and ploughing the lands." Back then, no matter whether they were noble or humble, the Chinese ideal of life was twofold: having pages and soil to turn. If a high-ranking minister chose to become a hermit, this was labelled as an instance of "retiring and returning to one's native place". A decorated general, after having achieved notable success, would "forsake his arms and return to the land". Now, notions have changed. If a general or a minister retires, the country rewards them with a pension, but not land. Currently, farmers are entitled to their own land. Nobody is without a patch, save for those whose birth violated the Family Planning regulations. If something is shared evenly, the inner magic of that entity decreases and eventually evaporates.

Commenting on the larger trend, the "farmer" of today is professionalised. The connotations of the word itself have changed. The ramifications are yet to be seen clearly and fully understood. "The construction of the New Countryside, the construction of the New Township" and the reform of the household registration system signify that the government is responding to change.

The idea of the land has evolved too. In earlier times, verse and prose extolled the joy of bucolic scenes, the affection of the smoke rising from the kitchen, and the "principal melody", which represented the core value of the time. The word "wayfarer" refers to one who has spurned his native place. The wayfarer's nostalgia is a kind of "principal melody" too. Notwithstanding, if writers today persist in writing like this it is branded out of date or out of keeping with the times.

Jia Pingwa's writing takes the land and the farmers as his main seedbed for observation. What he is drawing into focus is the series of paradigm shifts that have reverberated through the land in China. *Turbulence* was published in 1988. After that he wrote *The Abandoned Capital, White Nights, The Earthen Gate, Symptoms Report, Return to Old Gao Village, Missing Wolves, Shaanxi Opera,* and *Happy*. *Turbulence* was narrated from the position of the farmers. This is one of the limitations of that novel, though also a limitation shared by all writers in China at that time. Then, the term "mouthpiece" was very popular. Writers were mouthpieces. When they wrote about agricultural themes, they became mouthpieces for farmers. They became mouthpieces of an alternative kind when they wrote about industrial, military, and educational themes. That is to say, certain themes in novels compel the writers to assume particular positions.

Now, being a "spokesman" has become popular. Although there is a slight cadence between "mouthpiece" and "spokesman", the substitution of the former with the latter is ripe with significance. The spokesman for the Ministry of Education, the spokesman for the Ministry of Diplomacy, and the spokesman for the Bureau of Taiwanese Affairs, although each speaks about "partial interests", their positions have mutated. Their insights and angles of vision have changed. What they are talking about has a wider resonance and they are now discussing a "partial interest" from the perspective of the whole country.

After *Turbulence*, following the great labour pains of *The Abandoned Capital*, Jia Pingwa realigned his positions. From assuming the perspective of the farmers, he transferred his attention to the seams of Chinese culture. He critically observed the trauma and upheaval in contemporary life in the Chinese countryside. *The Earthen Gate* evokes the psyche of the farmers on the hinterland between the country and the city. That is to say, the frontier wherein the evolution of the idea of the land had been felt most keenly. It was a region full of anxiety. *Missing Wolves* envisaged the history of the wolves that dwelt in this altering land. "Wolf" referred to a person with very strong survival instincts. The novel instructed people on how to weather crises in which there was only a narrow escape route. *Symptoms Report* was a romance. In it, Jia Pingwa deliberately realigned his mode of narration, concentrating on how in the face of irrational forces humans plunge into the vagaries of their kind.

Return to Old Gao Village and *Shaanxi Opera* constitute a prelude; the rehearsals for a theatrical extravaganza, and the warm-up routines before a football match. Jia Pingwa is a director and a coach. He attempted many strategic possibilities in warming up. When the real match began, he chose the players for his side and the positions in which they should play. After the match, the audience paid attention to the result, but the coach preferred the warm-up because more of his wisdom and preliminary tactics were allowed to sparkle therein.

Happy represents a turning point in Jia Pingwa's writing. He started to construe a means of life for farmers ensnared in a dilemma of suffering. This novel bore the colour of "tomorrow". The parties in it subsist in a disfigured state, whereby the comedy is either superlatively deadpan or the characters are bereft of wit. Jia Pingwa's humour was bred in the bone. He could not clearly envision a way out for the farmers of contemporary China for he himself was beset with chronic worry and anxiety.

Under Jia Pingwa's pen, the Chinese countryside is of the minute. His novels have registered the unprecedented upheavals in the Chinese countryside. When it comes to the problems facing rural areas, he has been an independent and single-handed expositor and thinker. He has striven to lay bare the "rules", but I must say that until *Happy*, like other sociologists, he had not yet discovered them. If we express this through a fashionable saying, he was still "crossing the river by fumbling along the stepping stones".

Acknowledgements

The author and translators wish to thank Jamie McGarry, Jo Haywood and all at Valley Press for their assistance in bringing this book to fruition. Shaanxi Normal Publishing House granted copyright permission to translate the essays contained in this collection. Thanks are due to Dr J Graham Jones for assistance in proofreading.

Sponsorship was provided by First-class Universities and Academic Programs at Northwest University.